SAD LITTLE MEN

Also by Richard Beard

Fiction
X20: A Novel of (Not) Smoking
Damascus
The Cartoonist
Dry Bones
Lazarus Is Dead
Acts of the Assassins

Non-fiction
Muddied Oafs: The Last Days of Rugger
Manly Pursuits (or How to Beat the Australians)
Becoming Drusilla
The Day That Went Missing

Richard Beard

SAD LITTLE MEN

Private Schools and the Ruin of England

Harvill Secker
LONDON

5 7 9 10 8 6 4

Harvill Secker, an imprint of Vintage, is part of the
Penguin Random House group of companies whose addresses
can be found at global.penguinrandomhouse.com

Penguin
Random House
UK

First published by Harvill Secker in 2021

A CIP catalogue record for this book is available from
the British Library

penguin.co.uk/vintage

ISBN 9781787302938

Typeset in 11.5/16 pt ITC Galliard Std
by Integra Software Services Pvt. Ltd, Pondicherry

Printed and bound in Great Britain by Clays Ltd, Elcograf S.p.A.

The authorised representative in the EEA is Penguin Random House Ireland,
Morrison Chambers, 32 Nassau Street, Dublin D02 YH68

Penguin Random House is committed to a sustainable future for
our business, our readers and our planet. This book is made from
Forest Stewardship Council® certified paper.

MIX
Paper from
responsible sources
FSC
www.fsc.org   FSC® C018179

'... these people had the air of settling something: they either just had arranged or soon would re-arrange England. Yet the gateposts, the roads – he had noticed them on the way up – were in bad repair, and the timber wasn't kept properly, the windows stuck, the boards creaked. He was less impressed than he had expected.'

E. M. Forster, *Maurice*

Contents

Prologue

'Skools are not what they were in my day. Boys are no longer cruel to each other and the masters are friends.'
Geoffrey Willans, *How to be Topp*, 1954

I had a feeling I couldn't immediately place. I wanted to go out but wasn't allowed, except in strict measures of time. Shelves were emptying at the nearest supermarket, and instead of fresh fruit and vegetables I was eating British comfort food – sausages and mash, pie and beans. My freedom to make decisions like an adult was limited. I had homework I didn't want to do – a novel not going well – and I was lonely. I wondered when I'd see my mum again.

March 2020, first week of the first lockdown: I was fifty-three years old and felt like I was back at boarding school. Which wouldn't have mattered, but for the fact that at a time of national crisis my generation of boarding-school boys found themselves in charge.

I know how two of the last three British prime ministers were treated as children and the kind of men their schools wanted to make of them. My first night at Pinewood School was two days after my eighth birthday in January 1975. A term earlier David Cameron had left his family home for Heatherdown School in Berkshire, while also in 1975, at the age of eleven, Alexander Johnson was sent to board at Ashdown House in Sussex. The exact school picked out by the parents didn't really matter, because the experience was designed to produce a shared mindset, and about our Covid prime minister in particular I feel as Thomas Mann did about the leader of his country in the early 1930s. Whether I liked it or not, he was 'a brother – a rather unpleasant and mortifying brother. He makes me nervous, the relationship is painful to a degree. But I will not disclaim it.'

At the age of thirteen, after the preparation of the prep school, Cameron and Johnson progressed to Eton. I went on to Radley College near Oxford. I'm therefore a little out of bounds, without permission, but I'm old enough to risk that now and accept the consequences. Our parents were paying for a similar upbringing with a similar intended result: to establish our credentials for the top jobs in the country. In 1840 the founder of Radley, William Sewell, had dreamed of building 'a Winchester and Eton, and something more than Winchester or Eton'. Presumably not to emulate the brutality (in 1825 an Eton boy died after a fight lasting two and a half hours), but for the prime ministers. Between 1721 and 1900, of the thirty-two British prime ministers twenty-eight had been educated at English boys' boarding schools.

We followed a pattern. As small children we were sent away to school and in the summer went on family holidays

2

to Cornwall, because that was who we were or who we wanted to be. The tribal nature of the education was part of its appeal, and when in 1923 George Bernard Shaw advocated razing the public schools and 'sowing their foundations with salt', he meant the usual suspects – Eton, Harrow and Winchester – but also their 'cheaper and more pernicious imitators'.

In its defence, I don't believe Radley College was *more* pernicious. Nor in fact very much cheaper. But Shaw was right to see that this was recognisably the same kind of school in the same tradition. Sewell planned to build on an established recipe for success:

> [The English public school] has sent out into the legislature, into the Army, into the Professions, into the House of Commons, into political life, into the magistracy, into society generally, English boys with English minds, toned and trained to work with the machinery of the British Empire ... Our best men have been Public School men.

The newer, upstart Victorian public schools put into words, rather tastelessly, the assumptions that Eton left tactfully unspoken. And a hundred years later, by the end of the 1970s, the aims of these schools hadn't significantly changed. Public school men were still expected to dominate the sectors that Sewell identified, whether they were the best men for the job or not.

Today, much of the private school system has adjusted to phones and computers, to carpets and co-education and going home at the end of the long school day. But, to some degree, all anglophone private schools exist in the shadow of the institutions that influenced their founding. They replicate the segregation and social exceptionalism reserved for superior beings destined to lead. Private schools of various shapes and size, and not just in Britain, seek similar outcomes to Eton, Harrow, Winchester and Radley, which now stand alone as England's four enduring boys-only, boarding-only private secondary schools; the English private school in its purest form. These schools too will have tweaked and adapted, but to assume they change for the better is a tradition as old as the schools themselves, as described by Winston Churchill, here looking back at his childhood in the 1880s:

> Several grown-up people added that in their day, when they were young, schools were very rough ... But now it was all changed. School life nowadays was one long treat. All the boys enjoyed it. Some of my cousins who were a little older had been quite sorry – I was told – to come home for the holidays.

Churchill is joking, of course, his private schools were horrific. But in *My Early Life* he wrote about his education knowing the past was never dead. He chose to recall his resilience at prep school and Harrow to promote his qualities as a political leader. In that sense, the reality of these schools as they are today will only be felt in years to come, whereas now, in the early 2020s in the time of pandemic and Brexit, our leaders were moulded by the events and attitudes that characterised these schools in the late

1970s and early 80s. How those children survived then is the model for their survival now.

Pre-lockdown, to explore this idea, I'd have arranged research trips to match my personal experiences against those of Cameron and Johnson. I'd have emailed the headmistress of Ashdown House School (boarding available, co-educational), and using my private school charm ('it's all right, I'm one of us') I'd have invited myself to the school's 40 *acres of beautiful grounds* in East Sussex. On an afternoon in early summer I'd have occupied a corner of the sunlit library and worked through the old school magazines, searching out traces of Johnson the man in Johnson the boy. I'd have had a thoroughly enjoyable time of it, and stopped on my way out to watch some cricket. A few days later I'd have taken a morning train to Windsor, and crossed the footbridge over the Thames for face-to-face interviews with colourful characters in their natively revealing environment.

Unfortunately, in a pandemic neither Eton College nor Ashdown House are considered essential destinations, despite their influence on public life. During the lockdown I won't be going anywhere I can't reach on foot or by bicycle during my hour's permitted exercise.

According to Google Maps, now that I take the trouble to get a precise measurement, I discover I live exactly 0.5 of a mile from Radley College. That's three minutes on a bicycle. Which is, frankly, a fact I've been ignoring for the best part of five years. Of course I know the school is there, and about once a week I cycle past the main gates on my way into Oxford. I rarely give the place a second thought, because I have a firm grip on the sequence of events that led me to be living in Radley village, in a single man's flat at the top of a converted dairy and schoolhouse. Marriage, living abroad, having kids, moving back, finding a school on the other side of Abingdon with lessons delivered in French, divorce, moving out, not too far but with a train station for London. The steps make perfect sense to me.

The reasoning adds up, and the fact that I live in the village is coincidence. It's as much of a coincidence as when a man marries a woman with the same first name as his mother. It happens. Oedipus felt as unperturbed in Thebes. Honestly, how was he supposed to join the dots? His mother *and* his father. What are the odds?

So at first I dismiss this coincidental detail, as being insignificant. And although my schooldays from forty years ago seem far away, I have experience as a memoir writer with a bad memory. In my last book I reconstructed the drowning of my brother Nicky, a childhood trauma eroded by denial and time. Those corrosive factors have again done their work. According to Alex Renton, author of *Stiff Upper Lip*, the absence of a normal trove of memories is not uncommon in boarding school children as adults. Our brains become adept at organising a state of protective amnesia.

Luckily I'm used to scavenging for scraps, taking my prompts about the past from whatever sources make themselves available. In the absence of research trips I can still get books delivered (David Cameron, *For the Record*, £6 second-hand, 'signed copy, minimal wear,

VG+'), though I can't make a trip to the library (Boris Johnson, *The Churchill Factor*, no way I'm buying that). For Pinewood School, I have the research materials I foraged for *The Day That Went Missing* – letters and school reports and other salvaged ephemera from my mum's chaotic attic. I have a 1980 page-to-a-day diary, filled in from January until early April before, aged thirteen, I was distracted by the cricket season and a change of schools. Sometimes I feel fortunate to be the age I am, with my durable analogue childhood.

And despite physical isolation I have the internet. Thank God for the internet. Online resources include the Eton school magazine, called the *Chronicle*, which is digitised and open access for 1979–1984, as are the school magazines for Radley. After forty years of trying to forget, I realise how much help my memory needs when online I'm reacquainted with a visit to Radley College in October 1984 by the then prime minister, Margaret Thatcher. This was one week after the IRA bombing of the Grand Hotel in Brighton, and as a show of undaunted Tory strength, the government chose to parade its indomitability at an English boys' boarding school. We shall not be moved.

As for the reach of Google, no one is safe. I'll be contacting people who were there, if I can find them. I can always talk to my mum. I'll make full use of Wikipedia, for which I'm grateful and to which I've made a contribution. On YouTube, I find the complete series of the documentary *Public School*, directed by Richard Denton at Radley in 1979 and broadcast on BBC Television in 1980. *Public School* is an early reality show, and the ten-part series was so popular it inspired subsequent expeditions into the exotic unknown of boarding schools, films also accessible on YouTube as entertainment for all the family.

When I look through my shelves I see that over the years I've collected a number of books about English private schools, as if in anticipation of a national crisis that questions trust in the British style of government. I now have time to read essays and memoirs reaching back through the twentieth century, as well as the growing expert literature about the psychological impact of early boarding, pioneered in particular by psychoanalysts Joy Schaverien and Nick Duffell. George Orwell's shorter works are online in full, thanks to the Orwell Foundation, including his venomous essay about his days at a private prep school, 'Such, Such Were the Joys'.

'I base these generalisations on what I can recall of my own childhood outlook,' Orwell writes, 'treacherous though memory is.' I know, George, I know. I cling to Orwell like an emotional support author, but I worry he isn't totally cured of his education, his work mottled with boarding school displacements. 'However we may like it,' he writes in 'The Lion and the Unicorn', 'toughness is the price of survival.' I've therefore chosen two dead foreigners to be my elected objective guardians and guiding lights. From my shelves I'm pulling out Erving Goffman's *Asylums* (1961) and Hannah Arendt's *The Origins of Totalitarianism* (1951). For the purposes of this book, Aunt Hannah and Uncle Erving are the adults in the room.

Obviously I'm not just going to sit here. To stay healthy everyone needs their daily exercise. Usually, from my flat,

I jog a circular route down by the Thames. But in the second week of lockdown, in my allowed hour outside, I go looking for the public footpath through the school, which I haven't walked in five years of living here. The path isn't difficult to find. It goes straight through the main gate, passing a lodge house on the right which is now the base for the school's extensive security and surveillance set-up (*All areas on this site are covered by CCTV*). Outside the lodge in the sunshine, a middle-aged woman is sitting on a chair.

I keep two metres away and say hello. The woman works as a matron, and in the absence of boys the school is sharing out jobs to keep staff busy. This afternoon, Matron is on the security rota. She tells me that in the evenings, even though the boys are with their parents, she logs onto Zoom and they have virtual cocoa.

'But maybe you know that,' she says. 'Maybe you know the school.'

I can't quite bring myself to admit a connection. I pretend to be an innocent from the village, discovering the footpath as a bonus of lockdown. I don't say: I know this place, I'm from here, I was made here. The fact shames and weakens me, in ways I don't yet understand, and therefore by instinct I keep my schooldays a secret: the truth is I went to boarding school and I didn't like it. I'm sure I once read that line in a waspish book review dismissing the plot or the author of a hyped first novel. Now I can't find the source and wonder if I made up the criticism, and possibly the novel, to deter me from ever considering this kind of material. Self-censorship certainly fits the character type.

'Am I allowed to just come in?'

'Of course you are,' she says.

'Any time I like?'

'It's a public footpath.'

'So I could walk through here in the middle of the night?'

'If you wanted to. Not many people do.'

The path goes up the drive in a straight line. If I keep walking I'll end up well beyond the school and near the Oxford Road slipway for the A34. There's no circular path. It's up and back.

'Thank you,' I say, 'thanks very much,' because manners cost nothing.

The main drive is a gentle rise as far as a pair of red-brick memorial arches. On both sides there are new buildings I don't recognise, and rows of springtime chestnut trees in bloom. Inside the arches themselves the dead are drilled with precision – 219 names to the left (1914–18) and 220 names to the right (1939–45). The room directly above is a small chapel, where I once prayed to do well in my O levels. Out the other side, vast playing fields stretch to the right – the largest area of mown grass in England, or so we were told. Now the cricket pitches reach even further into what was once agricultural land, as far as the eye can see. Back at school as an adult, it's so much bigger than I remembered.

Keep walking; straight up, straight back. On the left is Shop and a view into the school past the Clock Tower, where a boy in his middle teens in jeans and T-shirt is riding a bicycle, round and round the Tower while humming to himself and ringing his bell. He looks too old for this. His body rocks forward and back as he pedals.

The buildings next on the left are A Social, a boys' boarding house. I nod at the windows of specific rooms where I used to live, and out of which I used to look. In the housemaster's garden, invisible behind a high trimmed hedge, a family has messed up the batting order and Mummy has missed her turn. There is discussion and disagreement. I move on and by a process of elimination pick out the ground-floor study where aged fourteen I had a cosmic revelation, understanding for a brief moment the structure and meaning of the universe. In the shrubbery between me and the study window, trees have been allowed to grow tall. Maybe they're study-bedrooms now. The boys of today need their privacy.

Past the History and German teaching blocks, past the Sub-Warden's house, down a slope to a lake on the left and the 400-year-old College oak on the right. I walk up through an avenue of beech trees that cuts through the school golf course, and at the top of the avenue sit down on the vacant seventh tee for a view back to the school. The golf course was here before 1914 and then again between the wars, but in 1980 we must still have been towards the end of the second post-war period of the century, stuck in the dug-up-for-potatoes period. The course opened again in 1985, and among my dad's files, the ones I rifled after he died, I found some 1982 school–parent correspondence. The headmaster, known as the Warden, sent Dad a note of thanks for his contribution towards the £100,000 golf course appeal, while reminding him to apply for the charity tax rebate.

Dad always wanted to belong. All his life he joined clubs – the Old Town club in Swindon, the Clarendon in Oxford, finally the East India in London. Not bad for a Swindon builder. Another note from his filing cabinet is my housemaster thanking him for dinner – *It was refreshing to be away from Radley with scarcely a schoolmaster in sight. I am really ready for the fray this morning!* As long as we joined the right clubs we'd be OK, and if that required donations and dinner invitations and sending his sons to this school, then so be it. That was the price worth paying.

Forty years later, I wonder if we ever belonged. According to the bursar's accounts we did, and not only because I have the receipts for the termly fees and the £12 original registration in 1975: *I have to ask that, if you change your address before that time, or decide to send your boy to some other School, you will be kind enough to let me know <u>at once</u>.* The tone was set, and at registration Dad was informed of the obligatory payments to the Radleian Society, meaning that *Boys on leaving School are elected to Life Membership of the Society without further subscription.* From the beginning I was expected to belong for life, without question. I was promised belonging to hurry Dad into making up his mind.

The top of the avenue is a lovely place to rest. Without the scurry of boys and the stress of teachers, the empty buildings are not so much a school as an idea, sitting plump and well kept in the cushion of the past. This is my territory as much as anybody's just now. On the walk back I pass Croome's Tower on my right and notice the door is open. I could walk into my old boarding house or through another double door into Paton's Quad and the Covered Passage, into the place names that suddenly light up for me.

I don't go in. Mainly for fear of infecting anyone, or being infected. But also I'm scared of getting told off – I'd be trespassing. The territory onto which I'm allowed is the past, which is famously another country, one accessible without travel restrictions. From what I remember of my schooldays, I can confirm they do things differently there, which is why most of this book is in the past tense. I know how things were then, between 1975 and 1984, the period that bred the men in power for the last decade who'd like very much to stay on for another, and who, whatever their ultimate fate, have influenced British politics into the foreseeable future.

If in hindsight our education seems unbelievable, the consequences are increasingly apparent. Fragile, entitled, in good times and bad we revert to what we learned as boys. But what was that, exactly? Forty years later those school-day experiences and attitudes have a magnified effect on the country, and in England it isn't difficult to look back and see where the nation's leaders were formed. This is a memoir about white middle-aged English public school boys. We have our reputation for a reason.

1

Habits for Life

'The manners and traditions learned by each class in child-hood are not only very different but – this is the essential point – generally persist from birth to death.'

George Orwell, *The Road to Wigan Pier*, 1937

Boris Johnson was born in June 1964, and David Cameron in October 1966.

I was born in January 1967 and my first political memory is of Mike Yarwood impersonating Prime Minister Harold Wilson on Saturday-night television. I knew the shadow of the prime minister but none of the substance. He had a pipe and a northern accent. Everyone laughed. Through the seventies I was vaguely conscious of the Labour Party's Wilson battling the Conservative Edward Heath to disown responsibility for the decade, with James Callaghan damping down a couple of less eventful years before the election of Mrs Thatcher in 1979. Always 'Mrs' Thatcher, like a headmistress too stern for a given name.

These four prime ministers – Wilson, Heath, Callaghan, Thatcher – were educated at grammar schools. The last patrician prime minister – Sir Alec Douglas-Home, son of Lord Dunglass and an Old Etonian – had been voted out of office by the great British public before Johnson was a year old, and before Cameron and I were born. By the 1970s we'd entered a new age, and wouldn't see another privately educated prime minister until Tony Blair in 1997, but he was Labour and his school was in Edinburgh so he didn't necessarily count. By 1997, in any case, I was practically married with a child on the way and school was a distant memory – I was beyond caring what school anyone went to, or so I believed at the time.

What I did know was that my first deeply felt political instinct had belatedly come true: in my heart, aged twelve, I was certain that Mrs Thatcher hadn't a hope of winning the 1979 general election. Not because she was a woman, but because the Conservative Party represented the interests of a class in decline, and I could be sure of this because I was in daily contact with Tory lifeblood at a private boarding school in a soft southern county of England. This was the class of people I was supposed to be joining, though not without reservations.

In my considered twelve-year-old's opinion the Conservatives were about to be swept aside by the tide of history, never again to secure a majority in Parliament. In reality, Mrs Thatcher triumphed and the Tories governed for the next eighteen years, winning four consecutive elections. Behind the walls of his prep school my younger self had mistakenly seen the ancient English certainties coming to an end, soon to be replaced by bolder alternatives. Looking back now I wasn't completely wrong, even though at the time I hadn't sat down to read the 1979 Labour Party Manifesto:

> Independent schools still represent a major obstacle to equality of opportunity. Labour's aim is to end, as soon as possible, fee-paying in such schools ... Labour will end as soon as possible the remaining public subsidies and public support to independent schools.

Or in other words, after my first four years in a fee-paying school I assumed the British public would vote for a fairer Britain. That seemed the rational choice, and it wasn't as if these schools were flourishing, as I knew from personal experience. In 1978 our Berkshire prep school was down to seventy-eight boys. In 1982, two years after Cameron left for Eton, his prep school closed down despite impeccable upper-class credentials. A press photograph of Heatherdown from the late sixties shows eight-year-old Prince Andrew on his first day shaking hands with the headmaster. I can't help but notice the Queen's hand in the small of Andrew's back, pushing him on, pushing him away. Fees, swelling with the decade's inflation, nearly doubled from £300 in 1975 to £550 by 1979 (and on the invoices, always 'payable in advance'). The only comprehensive school that Pinewood played at football, Carterton

Community College, beat us 11–1. The runes were there to be read, and the last rites to be administered. This was a system on its knees.

In 1973, the Labour Party had committed to what Shadow Education Minister Roy Hattersley called 'a serious intention to reduce and eventually to abolish private education in this country', a policy intended to capture a more general mood of change. An influential history of twentieth-century Britain published a year earlier was titled *The Collapse of British Power*, and towards the end of the decade Cameron's dad had emergency supplies stockpiled in his cellar. 'It sounds mad now,' his son writes in *For the Record*, 'but there were real fears of a military coup.' Evidently in the Old Rectory near Newbury there were. At about this time my mum sent me a letter with the news that my dad had lost his seat as a Tory councillor: *he says he doesn't mind but I think he does.* It felt as if an era was coming to an end.

Even to a child of twelve, by 1979 private education felt a beleaguered form of schooling. A dwindling number of parents saw the attraction of withdrawing small children from regular life for months on end, as if abducted by aliens, and leaving them in dormitories until their brains had been suitably modified. This rarefied experience was shared in 1978 by only 4.5 per cent of the population, and decreasing, because schools that were private and isolated would inevitably lose out to those that were public and comprehensive. Britain would become a more open, meritocratic nation that could look to the future with confidence.

18

Apparently not. Thirty years after my political epiphany, an Old Etonian former prep school boy was living in Number Ten, his children on the register for private schools of their own. Cameron was followed into Downing Street, after a brief interregnum, by another Old Etonian prep school boarder. Boys like me had snatched victory from the jaws of defeat. We must be pretty amazing, even if we thought so ourselves.

I know neither of these men personally. I do know that they spent the formative years of their childhood in boarding schools being looked after by adults who didn't love them, because I did too. Those of us who were there know what it was like, and if the character of our leaders matters then I'm in possession of important information. A potential prime minister, I too slept in schools from the mid-seventies into the early eighties. I had the same education as men who run the country.

Most of them are men. Going through Sewell's 1847 list of professions of influence today, the Army's Chief of Staff, Sir Mark Alexander Popham Carleton-Smith, is an Old Etonian, as is the editor of Britain's biggest-selling newspaper and the Archbishop of Canterbury. The Master of the Rolls and Head of Civil Justice, Sir Terence Etherton, was an early boarder at Holmewood House. Even Cressida Dick, the country's senior police officer, was at the Dragon School, Oxford, surrounded by the damage of early boarders, which at least equips her to deal with today's Chief Inspector of Schools and the Chief Medical Officer and the chairman of the BBC and the head of MI6. Boys like me, if we're not Conservative

19

life peers in the House of Lords, head up magic circle law firms and occupy the corner offices on the higher floors of international banks.

And as Sewell predicted, or at least hoped, public school men also remain conspicuous throughout the British government. Seventeen out of twenty-six members of Johnson's full Cabinet in 2020 went to private school. Of the more visible recent political buccaneers, the English private boarding school has sent out Rees-Mogg, Hunt, Mitchell, Cash, Redwood and Cummings: English boys with English minds.

Even the most famous of fictional public school teachers, Mr Chips, might have felt uneasy about this imbalance:

> Because always, whatever happened and however the avenues of politics twisted and turned, he had faith in England, in English flesh and blood, and in Brookfield as a place whose ultimate worth depended on whether she fitted herself into the English scene with dignity and without disproportion.

In the English scene, the influence of the private schools is disproportionate, and always has been. These exclusive schools, resistant to scrutiny, are responsible for traits that permeate the national sense of self, casting an excessive shadow. To understand how these traits develop is to illuminate a murky part of the national character, because public school boys are scattered like obstacles along every pathway to the top. Getting on can often mean imitating their way of being, and certainly involves dealing with it. This form of education is therefore everyone's inheritance, and appreciating how these people were made is to understand how England works, and why the country is in the shape it is. An insider would know, someone who was there.

For the full boarding experience, in the days when the powerful of today were mere children, two schools were involved. A prep school, where a boy started as young as seven, prepared boys to move at the age of thirteen to an entirely new set of buildings and friends at a larger public school. This public school was not 'public' in any ordinary sense of the word. In fact quite the opposite – the education was aggressively private, accessible to customers who had the cash. This wilful misuse of language, no matter the historical reason, could be addictive. Great Britain, United Kingdom, Public School. With time and repetition even simple words can slip their usual meanings. Private schools now prefer to be called 'independent', even though their existence depends on government-sanctioned charitable status, exemption from business rates and state training of their teachers. Old habits die hard.

Any differences in the 'independent' sector between prep school and public school were always less important than the similarities. Paul Watkins, a writer who was a contemporary of Johnson's at Eton (he had a feature in the school magazine that Johnson edited), writes in his 1993 memoir *Stand Before Your God* that 'much of what made sense there made sense here, even if it seemed to make no sense anywhere else'. Which wasn't strictly true, because

21

the codes and belief systems also made sense in the older Oxbridge colleges and in City firms and in legal chambers and in both Houses of Parliament. The boys from prep schools started their preparation early.

Whether it was Heatherdown or Pinewood or Ashdown, prep schools from that time had more in common with each other than not. If the school wasn't a House, it was likely a Hall or a Court. The customary look of the main building, as described by Roald Dahl, was 'private lunatic asylum', usually at the end of a drive and overlooking playing fields where the changing shape of goalposts marked the seasonal passage from rugby in the autumn to soccer and hockey after Christmas. Every year, at some point in April, the caged cricket square would be released from captivity. The package as a whole mapped itself onto an enduring English fantasy – the country house and grounds, with the house measurable in windows along and windows high. The setting, even then, was dedicated to a cherished but fading idea of England.

The public school followed similar principles though on a larger scale, for anywhere between 450 and 1,000 boys. Christopher Hibbert's history of Radley College, *No Ordinary Place*, recounts the search of a couple of mid-nineteenth-century oddballs, the double act of Sewell and Singleton, for an ideal school location that should resemble 'a private country estate'. They chanced upon Radley Hall near Oxford, built in the 1720s and complete with 136 acres of land.

Against these picturesque backdrops, nineteenth-century educational idealists offered boys from wealthy families as much beating and as little food as they could stand. In exchange for money. And amazingly this educational offer found its market, largely thanks to the unspoken promise of an outcome devoutly to be wished: prime minister, or near offer. For a stab at the best jobs in the country, a public school education was invaluable, and to secure a place at public school a prep school was where to start.

Among the Pinewood documents I salvaged from Dad's filing cabinets, I have a typed list from Spring Term 1976 with the addresses of the parents. The school roll that January was a meagre seventy-four boys. Like I said, hard times, but the names and titles are socially representative of a school like this at that historical moment. Two Revs, seven Drs, five Majors, a Lieutenant Colonel, a Lieutenant Commander, a Colonel, a Wing Commander, one Hon. These were the people who wanted the best for their children.

Of the humbler Mr and Mrs, I remember a farmer, a dentist, a solicitor and an estate agent. My dad ran a building company. About half the addresses are in the south of England; thirty of the seventy-four (including mine) are local, by which I mean driveable on a daily basis, if that's what the parents had wanted to do. The rest are randomly far-flung – Topsham in Devon, Dubai, Hereford, Atherton California, Northampton, Hong Kong, Kenya, West Sussex, Tehran, Paris, St James's Garden London, Summit New Jersey, Kuwait, Philippines, Kingston-upon-Thames, Poole in Dorset and Fairfax Station Virginia. These boys came together in term time and dispersed in the holidays, discovering from an early age the ins and outs of a double life.

Five of the Mr and Mrs couples have separate addresses, out of seventy-four opportunities for divorce. We always knew which parents were divorced, because their sons had the latest of whatever was newest. On the list is one boy of colour, who I see from his address lived not far from me in Swindon. At school we were in the same teams and he was a hero of mine: I can't remember once meeting up with him in the holidays. The demographic profile and geographical spread was likely to have been similar at public school, especially as there were government-subsidised places for the sons of army officers. As there still are today, at a cost to the taxpayer of about £80 million a year.

Both Pinewood and Radley educate more pupils now than they did in the late 1970s. Privately educated children today account for 7 per cent of the school population of England, though the percentage of boarders has decreased to a single per cent. In the twenty-first century these schools have changed in other ways too: they have counsellors and adequate heating, and white well-off English boys are exposed to the diversity of well-off children who aren't white, or aren't boys. They have dietary requirements.

On the other hand, the outcomes are assumed by parents to be broadly the same. Even without doubts about boarding or single-sex education, the academic and economic advantages of private school are today still weighed against the social and emotional hazards of an education that sets children apart from the wider community. On purpose. These children are being trained for leadership, or if not to lead then to earn. The most convincing reason to go to a private school remains to have gone to a private school, with the prizes that are statistically likely to follow. Want to be a senior judge? Sixty-five per cent of them had the same education that helped form almost half the country's newspaper columnists and two out of the last three prime ministers.

The prime ministers, at least, I can explain. I have the field guide to how they started out, which in 1975 meant among boys, at first very small boys in baggy shorts, scabs on our knees and ink between our fingers, if lucky with the brains for Latin and an eye for a ball. Then later, older boys at the slouch, hands in empty pockets because we had nothing left to lose, riding the early eighties on a wave of entitled arrogance.

It is noticeable, and often noticed, that something immature and boyish survives in men like Cameron and Johnson as adults. They can never quite carry off the role of grown-up, or shake a suspicion that they remain fans of escapades without consequences. They look confident of not being caught, or not being punished if they are. Cameron has his boyishly unlined face and Johnson his urchin's unbrushed hair, and his arch schoolboy's vocabulary. I'm boyish myself.

But what kind of boyhood was it, in our paid-for rooms in those repurposed mansions? What of the distant past still works in us as adults, and is it dangerous and can we pass the harm on to others? Are we the right people to steer the country, either clear of trouble or in the direction of sunlit uplands? The answer to these questions depends on lessons learned at an impressionable age. Unless, of course, we learned nothing. And no one pays hundreds of pounds a term, even in the late seventies, to learn nothing.

2

The Specific Period
1975–1984

'When I tell my children today about the schools I went to, and some of the things that happened in them, it all seems incredibly old-fashioned.'

David Cameron, *For the Record*, 2019

In 1975, for the boys in the private prep schools of the nation, World War II hadn't yet ended. The last two Japanese soldiers surrendered from their Philippines jungle in 1974, but small boys in uniform shorts in the converted country houses of England held out. In the House of Commons, private school boys of my generation continue to fight World War II even today.

Their background is absolutely to blame. Our schools were untouched by developments beyond the gates. HMT

Empire Windrush might as well not have steamed in from Jamaica in 1948, for all the difference its arrival made to Home Counties boarding schools. Industrial unrest and the oil crisis, for us, meant an inflationary rise in the weekly tuck allowance from ten to fifteen pence. It had no other impact. The IMF bailout and the three-day week and the emergence of feminism, let alone the tender family dynamics of popular paediatrician Dr Spock, were no match for polished shoes and a short-back-and-sides, in the 1970s as in 1945.

The biggest event in recent history remained the British winning World War II, mainly thanks to Churchill and the officer class. *We* won the war, alongside Kenneth More and David Niven, with the plucky Tommies (salt of the earth) forever indebted to the upstanding top brass. The teachers indulged this sentimental patriotism by allowing art classes to be used for model-making, so that Fairey Swordfish biplanes could repeatedly make a gluey mess of the Bismarck.

Our main source of war information was the trash mag, the small-format *Commando* comics that nobody seemed to buy but were always in circulation. The best of these have been reprinted in book form, in two volumes called *The Dirty Dozen, The Best 12 Commando Books Ever!* and *True Brit, The Toughest 12 Commando Books Ever!* The anthologies don't date the individual comics, but the cover art shows prices between five and seven pence, so they were written and published after decimalisation in the early seventies. We were the intended audience in that golden age of Bomber Command and the Desert Rats,

Spitfire aces and dour submariners in ribbed woollen hats. The only words worth saying were in capitals: JERRY EIGHTY-EIGHTS! NOW WE'RE IN TROUBLE.

In his introduction to *The Dirty Dozen*, editor George Low makes the point that many of the artists had seen active service. Their experience encouraged a house style that insisted on accurate portrayals of equipment and uniforms. The narratives were fantasies, but the style was a meticulous realism. The stories were lies, but they looked like they were true. And whatever political realism the nation's academics could push through London publishing houses, there was no *Collapse of British Power* in gutsy *Commando* comic books.

Berkshire in 1975 was at war. When the fields were waterlogged we group-walked the lanes and dive-bombed stones into puddles, then clattered survivors with machine-gun gravel. About once a year, as a treat, we played an outdoor game where the whole school separated into Fighters and twice-as-many Bombers. On each mission around the grounds the bombers took two metal bottle tops, hoping to deliver one as a payload into a drop zone. The other could be won by the fighters if they tagged a bomber on the way there or the way back. The only concession to the Cold War was the addition of a tennis ball, a nuclear strike worth a massive ten ordinary bottle tops.

No one was immune. A couple of years ago, when I ransacked my mum's attic, I found patchy evidence of my schooldays – not much, but enough material survived to be sure that the past actually happened. Inside a large-format *Silvine Drawing Book, British Made No 435*, is a series of pencil-and-crayon drawings of German warplanes defied by stickmen Brits shooting bombs individually out of the sky with their .303 rifles. A direct hit is signified by a bomb exploding in a frenzy of red crayon. Part of the pleasure was drawing swastikas on the Heinkels and Stukas, though some awkward erasing shows I'm uncertain whether a swastika starts down or across. Never mind, because despite the ack-ack flack the Germans have started unloading paratroopers, though on every page of the battle German casualties outnumber British by about five to one. Whatever the odds, the natural order of the universe prevails: the British always win.

'THEY HAD ME WORRIED FOR A MOMENT THERE, SIR.'

'YOU SHOULDN'T HAVE BEEN, SAM. THE SUBMARINE SERVICE NEVER FORGETS HER OWN.'

Images of combat and a patriotic imagination were as natural in this environment as breathing: the end-of-year art show was never complete without a sandy diorama featuring rubber tumble-weed and burnt-out German half-tracks. The best toy soldiers were the British commandos (green) with their Sten guns and woolly hats, though we were also partial to the 8th Army (beige) because like us they went about their work in shorts. The fumes from Humbrol paint and Britfix glue intensified the contribution of a million boy-hours to cementing victory over European neighbours.

YOU'RE WASTING YOUR TIME, JERRIES! WE'RE BIG BILL'S BOYS AND THEY DON'T COME ANY TOUGHER THAN US!

We were away from our parents and out of time. This was 1975 but it was also 1944, our schools preserved in an amber sometimes mistaken for gold. In the 1970s we experienced a style of education from at least twenty years earlier, when many of the teachers had learned their trade. The headmaster at Pinewood, Geoffrey 'Goat' Walters MA (Cantab), had started teaching at the school in 1942, though I now think our education would have been recognisable twenty years before that, and maybe twenty years earlier again. At Radley my piano teacher Miss Parkinson had sat beside her first public school pupil in 1925.

Mr Walters wore a small pre-war moustache, like the caricature of Teacher in the *Beano*. And, like Teacher, in the tradition of old-school headmasters, he kept a bamboo cane in his study. Thinking back to those days, my memory has been refreshed, tellingly, by books written well before my time. Words in common usage during my schooldays were brought back to me, for example, by E. M. Forster's *The Longest Journey*, published in 1907. This novel is about a Cambridge graduate whose student ideals are corroded when he takes a job in a provincial public school ('a gimcrack copy of Eton'), and Forster reminds me of our casual everyday Latin, which was exactly the same as his. Up to no good, we'd whisper *Cave!* – pronounced (by us) K.V! – Watch out!

As in Forster's day, the non-sporting boys were 'weedy', and at the end of a dispute two boys would officially ask, again in Latin, for *Pax*. Peace would usually break out. Forster could recall these details for me because the schools had barely changed. He summons up memories

31

of our public school dormitories with assigned cubicles, which had wooden partitions that didn't reach the ceiling and curtains for doors. E. M. Forster (born 1879) and I share similar memories of school, which is both ridiculous and true. His turn-of-the-century novel can provide an index of boarding school truths that hadn't changed seventy years later:

> *Day boys, mockery of*
> *Masters, frightfully tragic*
> *Patriotism, encouraged*
> *Portraits on the wall, Empire builders*
> *Prefects, house, school*

I find equally useful reminders in 'Such, Such Were the Joys', George Orwell's long essay remembering his prep school from the 1910s. Orwell too had compulsory Sunday letter-writing and the absence of fastenings on the toilet doors. And by the time I reach for Nigel Molesworth, the comic parody of an English prep school boy written by Geoffrey Willans between 1953 and 1959, I'm not just inhabiting an unchanging period I feel like I'm in the building.

St Custard's is from the same generic pool as Pinewood and Ashdown House and Heatherdown. By my calculations St Custard's has somewhere between sixty-two and ninety-nine boys, which is recognisably accurate. Molesworth is in a class of nine, and in one of my weekly letters home from 1977 I dutifully record the fortnightly order in which *I came second in a class of nine boys.* Molesworth's teachers wear black academic gowns, which might be imagined an exaggeration for comic effect, though in the BBC documentary *Public School*, from 1979, the self-regarding first-form teacher swirls into his classroom wearing a full-length crow-black gown.

Molesworth feeds me forgotten words once a part of everyday life: *swiz, blotch, grub, hard cheddar, sneak*. And, hesitantly, for a boy we happened to like: *Decent. Jolly decent*.

Molesworth and Johnson and Cameron and me, along with the editor of the *Daily Mail* and (picking another seemingly at random) the UK's Ambassador to the European Union, share a boyhood of naked swimming and no pants allowed beneath coarse woollen rugby shorts. The goalkeeper at soccer gets a grey Eton-collared jersey, while black leather football boots are dubbined on the Friday night before Saturday matches. During the summer evenings, after fielding practice, whitener is applied with a sponge to the knee rolls of canvas cricket pads. In 1977, part of Pinewood school did actually burn down, like in all the best school stories. According to the council report, 'the entire block was empty when the fire occurred as the boys were having tea at the time. The fire brigade was unable to state the cause of the blaze.'

In these details, the schools of the late seventies were more firmly attached to the years before than the years after. In 1980, at the start of term, Radley still sent the college lorry to meet the London train. The classrooms had blackboards and chalk dusters, and as remnants of Molesworth's England, at prep school we looked like Molesworth. Short trousers in grey corduroy all year round until the age of eleven. Grey shirts, blue ties and a grey V-neck sweater with a blue band, and on Sundays blue piping on the grey school blazer with a yellow-and-blue crest on the pocket. In Mum's attic I found a Pinewood school cap, size 6 ¾. Sewn into the lining, above the strip for a name tape, is a contact for the suppliers: *Gorringes of Victoria, Phone Vic.6666, London, S.W.1.* I'm fairly sure we had the same *School and College Outfitters* as St Custard's.

Molesworth, of course, is a legendary joker and life at school is a joke. His creator Geoffrey Willans and the illustrator Ronald Searle play the beatings for laughs, as they do the terrible food, but they didn't have the nerve to put everything in. No one would have believed them. Every morning after breakfast, before the quarter-mile walk down the drive and back, we had to line up in the changing rooms for Lavatory Parade.

Either side of the open showers were rows of toilets with half-size blue doors, a foot of fresh air at the bottom and the same again above shoulder height. If a boy was standing up, his head would be visible. These doors had no locks, and the favoured toilets had gloss paint thick enough to jam the door closed against the frame. Others had to be held shut with the clasp of an elasticated snake belt. Some cisterns, operated by an overhead chain, worked better than others. Every morning a teacher sat on a chair by the exit to the changing rooms, and as we filed out we had to say 'tick' or 'cross'. The teacher would then make an entry on a clipboard next to our name. We had no idea what this chart signified, so boys liked to set up a pattern. After a couple of weeks a line on the chart could make a pleasing

✔ ✘ ✔ ✘ ✔ ✘ ✔ ✘ ✔ ✘

Which then, after half-term, might change rhythmically to:

✔ ✔ ✘ ✔ ✔ ✘ ✔ ✔ ✘ ✔

Or even:

✘ ✘ ✘ ✔ ✘ ✘ ✘ ✔ ✘ ✘

Any boy feeling brave or down in the dumps might experiment with weeks of determined consistency:

✘ ✘ ✘ ✘ ✘ ✘ ✘ ✘ ✘ ✘

As far as I know, none of these patterns were ever questioned or had any consequences, even though the Bog Parade was a system for monitoring bowel movements. Whatever the invented or real sequence, the parade wasn't about health but about power. As was the arbitrary patterning of our results. The teachers were playing a game; so were we.

These power games quickly became standard behaviour, whether having to stand up for teachers entering a room, or observing dress codes for different times of day or places. In hindsight we were living, every day, a period re-enactment. At Radley, our cubicles were recognisably the same basic design as those in a photo of the Long Dormitory from 1849. Shop was pretty much unchanged from a drawing of 1947, and we continued the 1950s practice of reading a passage of scripture every day before the beginning of first period, whatever subject the class happened to be.

We took our places in an England theme park with almost accurate historical costumes (some dolt usually forgot to remove a digital watch, or his aviator specs). Our collective recreation of an idea of England featured the Great House with grounds and staff, the joy of Sten-gunning a foreign intruder and the unreality of a life without cars. We merged with the past, assiduously protected from *modernity*. Which, as a side effect, kept us safely insulated from contemporary Britain. Tom Brown's schooldays at nineteenth-century Rugby were more relatable to us than Tucker's troubles at TV's Grange Hill.

Our intimacy with history also included a kind of ancestor worship. Paul Watkins, the Eton contemporary of Johnson and Cameron, describes the impact of an early day at Eton listening to the headmaster in 'a long hall over the main entrance to the school courtyard'. He was not going to a new school, but to a very old school – the New Buildings at Eton date from 1846 – and at first Watkins finds himself distracted by the marble busts in the hall. The old boy prime ministers and grand Empire statesmen make him feel the pressure of his parents' paid-for expectations. He senses the ambition not just of his peers but of every boy with experience of that room for the last five hundred years. He will have time to dwell on how best to make his mark. 'The great steamroller of time stalled when it reached Eton.'

By the 1970s, even the newer public schools could manage a decent job of stalling time. Radley Hall had been sketched by Turner in 1789, and in 1947 the guests at the school's centenary included young Princess Elizabeth and Field Marshal Montgomery. The school amassed history and belonged to history, and wanted us to feel implicated in the nation's historical destiny.

The lingering rituals – the fancy dress, the shared study rooms so small there wasn't space for a desk, only a board over the arms of a chair – conflated time, so that school for us was essentially the same experience as it had been for a century. Similar outcomes were anticipated, yet the future looked increasingly alien and unfamiliar. From the pre-mechanised twentieth century, at about teatime on a clear day in Berkshire, we could watch Concorde on its descent along the M4 corridor towards Heathrow.

A 1981 letter from the new headmaster at Pinewood (himself a boy at the school from 1947 to 1952, so every update was relative) notes the changes to come: 'we would very much like to heat the swimming pool. In addition we plan to improve the central heating system and the over-crowded changing-room facilities, if funds permit'. The cold and unsanitary conditions couldn't last forever, but none of those changes had yet taken place.

At school on the far edge of yesterday, we linked arms back to Nigel Molesworth and George Orwell and E. M. Forster, but we also found ourselves on the cusp of the unknown. We were the first point of contact with electronic calculators and digital watches. The generation before us could claim direct experience of the challenges of war, the real one. The generation after had Childline and the 1989 Children Act, which in accordance with the UN Convention on the Rights of the Child placed a legal duty on private boarding schools to 'safeguard and promote' pupil welfare. Better late than never, but the leaders we have in this country now were made in schools before safeguarding, when parents paid for the privilege of unsafeguarded children.

In his preface to the Penguin Classics edition of *Molesworth*, Philip Hensher sees that the books 'reflect their period, which is that of the fifteen or so years after the second world war, thoroughly, and gloriously'. But what was different, another fifteen years later? On the surface, very little. We wore short trousers and wrote with leaky fountain pens and swam naked in an unheated pool and shared Molesworth's boyish enthusiasms for spaceships and Romans and war and dinosaurs. The social upheavals of the 1960s might as well never have happened: we were preparing in the traditional way for an England that for most other English people had changed, and which with the arrival of the silicon chip was about to change still further. So what exactly were we?

The answer – stubbornly, hopefully – was that we were what we'd always been. The instinct of these schools was to hide in a glorified past. As an example of the safe space of history we were small boys who revered Churchill, who as a small boy himself had been alarmed by the liberal radicalism of Gladstone. In our version of history rewritten as medication – mood-enhancing, but also tranquillising – all dead Victorian politicians became honorary Conservatives. Gladstone too was one of us, because he couldn't ruin anything now. Even Winston's father, Randolph, became an honorary adult, and in *My Early Life* a photograph shows him wearing a huge moustache in the serious disguise of the times. Victorian public school boys, too, could get stuck at boyish, but made more use of facial hair to grow themselves up.

I think we knew that change was coming, because nostalgia clung to the experience even as we lived it. Sprinklers caught the low summer light across the late-evening cricket square. In bed by 8.15, long before nightfall, I watched the high white clouds as they lazed across the country. In summer terms the sunlight after lights out was everywhere, so much light, into the far corners of the room and among the dust motes under the beds. That evening golden light is my favourite colour, when at the end of the day England turns its face to the sun.

Why was I among the dust motes, under the bed? It was some kind of game, but if caught out of bed after lights out I'd get beaten, because that's what happened in 1975 as it had since English schooling began. I can't remember why I wasn't wearing clothes.

The 'newer' Victorian public schools were seeded by the British Empire, a reason for their existence sunk deep into the lived experience. Rex Warner, author of the novel *The Aerodrome*, writes in his 1945 history of public schools that from the Victorian perspective 'the public school boy of the future was to be equipped with the knowledge required for entrance to Sandhurst or to the Home or Indian Civil Service'. Historically, if the role of prime minister was unavailable, we were being trained for a life administering Britain's overseas possessions, and to do a decent job of that it helped to subscribe to the uncomplicated attitude of star-colonist Cecil Rhodes: 'We are the finest race in the world and the more of the world we inhabit the better it is for the human race.'

The influence of Empire, surviving well into the 1970s, often went unrecognised and unacknowledged. Male circumcision serves as an example. Among upper-class families, circumcision had been a health fad at the beginning of the twentieth century, prompted by dusty Empire adventures in the Middle East, along with humidity issues nearer the tropics. By the 1930s, two-thirds of boys in the leading public schools were circumcised, and because English society moved slowly, this was still true by the late 1970s for about half the boys in the Pinewood showers. We had no idea why this should be, and although we noticed the difference we considered it as arbitrary as brown versus blue eyes. Or in this case, because English history provided a universal frame of reference, Roundheads versus Cavaliers.

Even for us, living behind the times, there was no judgement in this distinction – the animosities of the English civil war had thankfully cooled. Instead, the ideal private school education would instil the positive qualities of the Puritans – moderation, piety, good manners – *and* the advantages of the aristocracy – panache, entitlement, hereditary leadership. English history could be refashioned like this to console us; we could have our cake and eat it. The heroes of our selective version of history were Francis Drake playing bowls, Nelson seeing no ships and Wellington victorious at Waterloo via the playing fields of Eton. We favoured Battles of Britain that saved Europe for freedom and democracy, proving that because we were English we were special; we were *exceptional*. Whatever the historical question, British national destiny was the answer.

On Saturday nights the school sometimes rented a film, which the whole school watched in the assembly room on blue leatherette seats, fixed together in rows of four. At any shocking moment, the connected rows lurched back as one. The film reels arrived inside aluminium canisters, and a technically minded boy took responsibility for setting up the ancient projector. The films available and affordable in this format were limited. We watched repeat showings of *Zulu*, *The Guns of Navarone*, *Waterloo*, *The Wooden Horse* and *Young Winston*, none of which challenged our partial version of history.

With a small adjustment, a minimal turn of the head, this glorified national past could stand in for our personal past, a vacated space now that memories of family and home were discouraged and felt irrelevant to our daily lives. In the place of any ambition to love, or be loved, we dreamed of fulfilment as upright British heroes, governor generals or Captains of the Horse. In our theme-park schools the theme was glorious Britain, artificially enriched in our unformed souls like a lab experiment that foreshadowed a future dystopia. At the end of Empire, indoctrinated Empire schoolboys refused to die.

We became sentimentally involved in the national story, just like boys with our education a century earlier. Jingoistic Etonians had written the music to 'Rule Britannia' and 'Jerusalem', and the words to 'Land of Hope and Glory'. Thanks to them, we had sacred music to soundtrack a holy past of valour in adversity (the Battle of Hastings, Dunkirk), vigour as plucky underdogs (Agincourt, the Armada), and a stubborn determination to uphold our values and never surrender (colonialism, the two world wars). Looking more closely we were also angels of moderation (13,000 French prisoners untouched after Blenheim), despite the assembly of awesome armies from the Battle of Malplaquet onwards. These outbreaks of virtue we likewise accepted as a national and therefore personal characteristic.

Of the many examples of perfidious Albion, Britain's history of lies and betrayal and arrogance and cruelty and rapaciousness and snobbery and corruption, few featured in our orange cloth-bound pamphlet 'Pinewood School History for Common Entrance'. The fact above all others that ignited our boarding school pride was that this plucky island nation of ours hadn't been invaded since 1066. We were small, isolated, but we knew how to look after ourselves. It was a story with intense personal resonance.

Until at least our teenage years we had less of an idea about what was happening in the present tense. Our intake of news at Pinewood was the responsibility of a different 12-year-old boy each week, who left breakfast early to sit in an empty classroom with a buzzing valve radio. The light from the dial was cream on sepia, and one of us would hunch up close and listen, pen in hand, to the 8 a.m.

bulletin on Radio 4. We'd then read out our summary of world and domestic events at assembly, which was held in the glass-roofed Orangery that connected the main house to a corridor of classrooms. On a good day, if all went well and the rain wasn't hammering on the glass, we heard at most a couple of minutes of current affairs, including the latest from Northern Ireland or the war in Rhodesia. The luckier newsreaders got a football or cricket score to report, to be shared out in loyal BBC English, with the rhythms as immutable as the shipping forecast.

Manchester United nil (rising tonality, pause), *Everton* (neutral, evenly spaced syllables, falling slightly) *nil.*

The defeat of the Spanish Armada felt more pressing than world affairs – we'd be tested on that, and would want to do well. School was the narrow world that mattered, and of the big news events of my early childhood I remember the death of Elvis Presley (1977), the Queen's Silver Jubilee (also 1977), the lead-up to Mrs Thatcher's election (1979) and the marriage of Charles and Diana (1981). These stories had to happen in the holidays or they wouldn't have registered, which partly explains why cricket could grip so fiercely the imaginations of boarding school children. It was a sport we could follow uninterrupted on television during the summer holidays, a rare lengthy stretch when we were in the same time zone as the rest of the country. Cricket rooted us into at least one shared experience with everyone else.

The exception to this effective blackout was the Falklands War (1982) which by special dispensation we were allowed to follow on TV news bulletins. Because, well, war. We were interested in Britons marauding over the globe with the Empire imperative 'to put things right', especially as our history lessons and the *Commando* mags had taught us what to expect: the British would end up winning. What a terrible outcome that was, in the long run, for its influence on impressionable and isolated minds. Rule Britannia, Britannia rules the waves.

3

Tough Guys

'The English privilege was obtained by hardship, and the best hardship was to be found at English boarding schools.'

John le Carré, *A Perfect Spy*, 1986

According to their own mythology, English private boarding schools bred the finest men on the planet who until very recently had governed a fifth of the world's population and a quarter of the Earth's land mass. While at school, however, these men as boys had individual possessions no bigger than the pockets in a small boy's shorts. A clothing list told us what we needed, and that was what we had. Our stipulated wardrobe included the Harrods-supplied shorts and shirts of prep school and the sports jacket and shirt 'of sober pattern' for public school.

'Polishable shoes, not boots', and regulation gentlemanly essentials:

    1 hairbrush and comb
    1 sponge bag
    1 shoe-cleaning kit
    1 pair of nail scissors

Aged eight, we were also allowed one soft toy, name-taped as proof of ownership. My mum showed her rebellious streak by sewing me a Kanga from *Winnie-the-Pooh* with Roo in the pouch. I therefore had two soft toys that passed as one, though Roo was mostly used as an indoor rugby ball. Otherwise, under the hinged lid of an allocated desk, our belongings included Philip & Tacey exercise books and a school-issue Platignum fountain pen, kept in a tin with our Helix Oxford Mathematical Instruments. The metal lid we customised with a compass point. In the pigeonholes outside the dining room we each had a napkin in a stainless-steel ring engraved with our initials (itemised at £1.25 on the Matron's Account, March 1975). We had a space in the changing room and a bed in the dormitory. These territories that were ours were undisputed, but they were also very small.

As were we, at the beginning of both schools and in comparison to the older boys. Historically, boys suffer at private boarding schools. Our period of the late seventies and early eighties, in private school time, was the late stages of an era connecting back to 1950, which in turn connected to 1930, and so on, staying within touching distance of boarders dying in fights or from savage beatings. By the end of the seventies the severity was milder (it *was* worse in their day) but the principle remained the same: without suffering, without pain, boys couldn't be turned into hardy Englishmen sound and true.

This belief amounted to a philosophy, a theory of human nature in the bloodstream of these institutions: boys should be ruled by fear before they could be guided by affection. Radley College was founded in 1847; the first boy was whipped within a week. His name was Alexander Clutterbuck and he was nine years old. Poor Clutterbuck. He was a repeat offender, and of a later beating the school's co-founder Robert Singleton wrote:

> So I got a good hazel switch, and laid it about him pretty soundly. He spun like a cockchafer, and shrieked like a sea-bird, and, as punishment was inflicted in a large empty room, the sound was magnified and prolonged ... Reynolds [a teacher], I hear, was in fits laughing at his screams.

At Pinewood Geoffrey 'Goat' Walters was a beater. He used a slipper for trivial offences and a cane for more serious misdemeanours. Beating was tolerated because it was traditional: Roald Dahl's memories of his 1930s schooldays, as told in *Boy*, revolve around the many times he was beaten, and in those days the practice was morally acceptable to the point that his vicious Repton headmaster, Geoffrey Fisher, later became Archbishop of Canterbury. By any standards, these schools were slow on the uptake

– in Europe, Erasmus had opposed corporal punishment in the sixteenth century. And when beating was finally banned in UK state schools in 1987, private education chose not to follow until 1999, perhaps shamed into action by the imminence of the twenty-first century.

Cameron was beaten. He says so in *For the Record*, 'with the smooth side of an ebony clothes brush'. Unsurprisingly, Johnson was also beaten, which he remembers with a common word of the times, 'whacked'. These were the traditions into which we were fed, but beating was by no means the only indignity.

From my desk, I pay my first visit to Erving Goffman, a Canadian-born sociologist with chairs at Berkeley and the University of Pennsylvania. He died in 1962, aged sixty, but in his Wikipedia picture he welcomes me into his black-and-white study, his hands clasped professorially over a flurry of manuscripts, fingers interlaced. He has a kind smile for a well-intentioned stranger; he doesn't get up.

I bow slightly and sit in a chair that's lower than his – Goffman is the sixth most-cited author of books in the humanities and social sciences, behind philosophers Michel Foucault and Pierre Bourdieu but ahead of Jürgen Habermas. These things are important to people like me: *I came 4th in a class of 15 boys.* Professor Goffman also has an interesting sister, an actor who played the Fonz's grandmother in *Happy Days* and who was later a favourite of David Lynch.

'Your sister was excellent in *Twin Peaks*,' I say, attempting to ingratiate myself. 'She was also outstanding in *Blue Velvet* and *Wild at Heart*.' Except Goffman died before those movies were cast, living on for my purposes in his second published book, *Asylums*, which examines the mechanics of what he calls 'total institutions'. His room at the University of Pennsylvania is papered with citations, like certificates:

> A total institution is a place of work and residence where a number of similarly situated people, cut off from the community for a considerable time, together lead an enclosed, formally administered round of life. The concept is mostly associated with the work of sociologist Erving Goffman.

Among his definitions of a total institution, Goffman lists a category 'purportedly established the better to pursue some workmanlike task and justifying themselves only on these instrumental grounds: army barracks, ships, boarding schools, work camps, colonial compounds, and large mansions from the point of view of those who live in the servants' quarters'. Inhabitants of a total institution can be of three types: voluntary, semi-voluntary and involuntary. At an English boarding school, at different times the children will be all three, but the world they enter is enclosed and has much in common with the asylum at Bethesda, Maryland, where Goffman did most of his research: 'in our society, they are the forcing houses for changing persons; each is a natural experiment on what can be done to the self'.

As in all total institutions, at boarding school the break with home has to be fully achieved before a child can embrace this new life and the lessons it has to offer.

Goffman explains that 'admission procedures might better be called "trimming" or "programming" because in thus being squared away ' – meaning primed by separation for whatever happens next – 'the new arrival allows himself to be shaped and coded into an object that can be fed into the administrative machinery of the establishment, to be worked on smoothly by routine operations'.

The 'trimming' didn't need to be horrific, just effective, and it started with the uniform. After the holidays we always went back to school in the late afternoon, even though our instinct for the rhythms of normal life flagged this as the wrong time of day for beginnings, let alone school. The shirt collars itched and the shorts were not what we'd have chosen to wear. The long woollen socks, held beneath the knee by name-taped elastic garters, were another required accessory for the next three months of period re-enactment. Always, we had a smart new haircut for a new term, and as a result, as adults, some of us vowed never again to be told what to do with our hair. We were transformed like this three times a year, made to dress and act like a different person, someone who wasn't us. Personal transformation became as natural as the seasons.

The uniform and the haircut anticipated the renaming. Beard. Johnson. Cameron. In the sixties at Pinewood a future Duke of Marlborough and imprisoned substance abuser was called 'Blandford'. The name he used when simply himself was Jamie. At Eton, the Princes William and Harry became 'Wales'. Each boy was now a family name and not an individual.

Whatever our parents did (builder, stockbroker, EU bureaucrat, hereditary peer) we wore the same collar and tie, starting afresh as schoolboys first and foremost. It was egalitarianism, of a sort, and social distinctions on the outside became immaterial because at school everyone had the same amount of money, ten pence a week on account for sweets on Saturday evenings. Overnight, we were supposed to turn from children into little men, and I owned my first leather briefcase at the age of thirteen, a requirement on the clothing list for public school where our costumes grew more ornate, almost ironic – at Eton the white tie and tails, at Radley an awkward short black gown for lessons and chapel. We remained as showily resistant to contemporary reality as Orthodox Jews.

Trapped at school we had rules to learn, many of them absurd, so that regulations functioned as they often did for the Soviets, not necessarily to make sense but as a reminder of who was in charge. No long trousers until the age of eleven. Jackets must be worn in Covered Passage on weekdays. Those two I remember. Here's one from the 'Radley College School Rules' that I found in Dad's papers: *No Colours ties may be worn on Gaudy or Sunday.* Obviously. And another: *No boy may sing, whistle, run or have his hands in his pockets in the Cloisters.* These are the kind of rules that E. M. Forster's fictional teacher lost his soul enforcing, in 1907.

But enforced they must be. At public school, second time round into a new total institution, we had to sit a new boys' test to check we could distinguish the teachers by their initials and identify the meaning of differently striped ties. We needed to memorise the names of the prefects and where was out of bounds, and however we'd previously self-identified we were now known as *stigs*. No one knew why; it was traditional. These rules were the new reality, and loyalty to other rules from earlier schools or at home should be disregarded – a change of allegiance was another habit detoxified for life.

This second humbling happened aged thirteen, rather than at eleven when most children start at secondary school. On the cusp of adolescence, a new start at the bottom of the pile was harder to take. Anger was closer to the surface, as was the seething unspoken promise that someday, somehow, someone would have to pay.

On a fine day in springtime, in the twenty-first century, Radley College can be picture-perfect. On either side of the drive, in between the chestnut trees, strips of grass are left unmown to encourage wild flowers – cow parsley and buttercups and bluebells. May sunshine softens the red brick of the memorial arches, above which the school flag laps gently in the breeze. The crest has a snake on it, affiliating us to the Slytherins. *Sicut serpentes.* Be wise, sure, but as wise as snakes.

At the start of the summer term the school is completely empty of this year's complement of 680 boys. During a pandemic this kind of boarding school doesn't contain the child of a single key worker, it would seem. Some of the staff, like the archivist, are on furlough, and in this ghost state the school waits in its pristine complacency, the outer manifestation of a superior mind, the neat dead heart of

England. The immaculate buildings and grounds feel like the incarnation of a Tory public announcement: 'We're right, everyone else is wrong, aren't we doing well?' The school is doing very well. In the theme park there's no graffiti, no litter, and this beautifully preserved acreage of England asks me to grasp the futility of setting myself against it.

I notice from the footpath that many of the newer buildings are rounded. The new science block to the left of the drive is round. Rounded stairwells soften the ends of the new teaching block to the right, and just before the memorial arches there's a sign for the Round Pavilion. It feels like an effort, conscious or otherwise, to smooth off the edges of what institutional psychiatrists sometimes call the 'brick mother'. As for other stand-in parents, the current Warden crosses the drive ahead of me and strides purposefully towards the Music School and tennis courts. He's looking relaxed in an open-necked shirt and quilted gilet, and I recognise him because several years ago I was asked to judge the school Declamations competition. I sat in the 300-seat school theatre with my only conscious prejudice, at the time, against boys who recited poems from the First World War.

But honestly, the school as it is now isn't my chief area of interest. This Warden is three Wardens on from when I left, and I've no logical reason to feel strongly about a pale-complexioned stranger with upstanding white hair. Yet the sight of him sets up a chattering seismograph of anxiety. I don't introduce myself because I don't want him to know who I am. Behind my cap and sunglasses, my Covid beard, I don't want to be found out or to be caught. My heart beats faster: the most unforgivable crime is to sneak, worse even than blubbing. Telling tales will not be tolerated, even though in most cases it meant telling the truth.

And breathe. The Warden has safely passed by. Easier as an old boy not to remember too much, the good bits excepted, often involving cigarettes or cricket. But I did like some of it. I was lucky. I was good at the stuff that mattered – at lessons, emotional repression and rugby. I was adaptable to the dodging and weaving, and even cynical Molesworth sometimes got emotionally confused: 'Goodbye headmaster goodbye peason acktually you are jolly d. and it is sad to leave. Goodbye to all goodbye.'

I can't speak for the boys of today, and I won't. We'll find out how the experience was for them in a few decades' time, possibly too late, from what happens to state education and NHS hospitals and other public services their parents currently pay to avoid. In the future, as now, it may seem absurd that a boy from a boarding school like this one should seek recognition as a legitimate representative of the people. How could we know anything of the Great Britain outside these walls, without making an immense effort from the day we left to work on nothing else but that? Look at today's public school leaders and public school prime ministers, and consider whether this is an effort they've made.

By now I'm a lockdown regular on the public footpath, and after the memorial arches and Shop I stop at the vista that opens up between the Clock Tower and the Rackets

Court, towards the Arts Centre and either C or D Social, I can't remember. The boy on his bike finds different routes and loops around the Tower. He rings his bell, he hums a tune. I try to remember what else I can't see from here. The red-brick chapel, the covered passage which was supposedly the longest corridor in England – we were always ready to believe in our connection to the biggest and best. First-class; world-beating. Signs say *Clock Tower Court* and *Sewell Centre Gallery*, a nod to the school's founder and a reminder that the past is always present.

Which it is. Christopher Hibbert attributes to Sewell, with historical hindsight, the 'streak of the charlatan', and in 1945 George Orwell himself reviewed a biography of Radley's founder: 'If he is now forgotten, this book, which is mostly a mass of ill-digested documentation, is not likely to make him less so, but the author does show good reason for thinking that Sewell, as much as, or even more than Arnold, was responsible for giving the public schools their present character.' Which, to put the two observations together, takes the charlatanism from the man and transfers it to the schools, to this school and others like it.

Further along I stop at an arch in the teaching block (Classics and Theology) that frames a view beyond lawns of the original eighteenth-century mansion house. Radley Hall, as was, is a classically proportioned red-brick block of a stately home, eight windows along and three windows high. The Whipping Room, which Singleton described as large and empty, was in there somewhere, behind one of those windows. 'To this hour,' wrote Sewell in his memoir, his nineteenth-century headmaster's *For the Record*, 'some of the most delightful, touching, blessed associations I have are connected with the whipping room at Radley.'

Despite the calculated roundness of recent building work and the happy boy on his bike and the extraordinary facilities (real tennis before breakfast, sub aqua and beagling after tea) I never mistake the school for a holiday camp. Sewell and Singleton's Whipping Room exists, fixed into the fabric of the place. It survives in the cultural memory of this type of education, in the psychogeography, in the pyscho-interior design, the psycho-floorplans, as a psychohistorical fact of this bastardised country estate.

I come here nearly every day now, to feel for the facts of the past and how they shape the present. It strikes me as important work, because this and schools like it fashioned the decision-makers responsible day by day for increasingly consequential decisions. And also because this was the place that happened to me. I want my experience of separation and fear to have had meaning, or it was such a fucking waste.

In the early eighties the Radley Warden Dennis Silk was a beater, or had been until recently. Appointed in 1968, by 1982 beating was much on his mind. He wrote to the parents to clarify his thoughts:

> You may wish me to say something on the presently fashionable topic of beating ... I find myself less inclined to use it now as a punishment and in fact have not beaten a boy for about five years. I feel that this is partly due to a

56

growing distaste in me for beating as a form of punishment and also partly from the fear that if it should ever go wrong in any way the 'press hounds' would love a juicy 'beating story'. If any of you have strong views on it one way or the other do get in touch with me, but I can see a moment when the punishment will have faded away rather like flogging in the Navy with a cat-o-nine-tails. It has simply gone out of fashion.

Like flared trousers, it wasn't wrong but it sent the wrong messages. It wasn't wrong but it could 'go' wrong, and only the Warden knows the pictures he had in his mind. By the early eighties beating children just didn't look right. In one of his many interviews during the BBC's *Public School*, Silk looks directly at camera: 'A little bit of fright doesn't do them any harm.'

More often, amid the grey sulks of adolescence, the fright came in the form of 6 a.m. runs and a horrible punishment involving a bath with no plug; we had to block the plughole with a heel and turn on the cold water. An older boy watched until every part of the naked body was immersed. But a beating would have been worse. In the film *Young Winston,* the future prime minister is beaten while his assembled prep school listens in. Even Winston Churchill cried, when he was small and sad and alone.

At Pinewood, boys waiting to be beaten sat on the lower steps of the polished wooden staircase of the main house. At the foot of this staircase was the door to the headmaster's study, and boys were not allowed to use these stairs at any time for any other purpose. That was a perk for masters. For going upstairs to the dormitories, we used the back stairs beside the kitchens.

When I visited the school in 2015, I found it hard to get my bearings. Rooms in the main house had been reconfigured with false walls, and corridors rerouted like pathways in a new brain that didn't make sense to me. The main entrance and huge open reception room, however, were unchanged, and even in 2015 the staircase filled me with dread. Boys and girls were freely using the stairs to get to their classrooms (now in the place of the unused dormitories) and my first instinct was to shout out a warning. '*Cave!* Get off the steps! Quick! Are you all *mad*?' There was no greater crime than disrespecting the privileges of others.

Walters used a length of bamboo. Although none of us liked to be punished, we all wanted to have been beaten, as a mark of honour. A caning had more kudos than the more common slippering, and while pride had its public moment the shame and humiliation were buried, sunk into the deep alongside other uncomfortable emotions. I was caned because Walters found me hiding after lights out under the bed of another boy, without any clothes on. It was one of those fully-lit summer evenings. I was trying to get my pyjamas back. I can't remember how my pyjamas came to be missing.

The headmaster took a dim view. The next day at the end of breakfast, as was the custom, he stood up and announced to the assembled school that Beard would go and sit on the steps. While I waited, boys walked past from breakfast to the classrooms, and in his secretary's office Walters warmed up, his cane hitting the padded back of a chair. I minded the physical pain and the bruising, but the longer-term distress came from not knowing what I'd done wrong. Maybe there were headmasterly hints against sexualised 'beastliness', but I missed that angle at the time and I still wouldn't have understood what he was talking about – the disgust was his not mine.

Without knowing it, I was living through an early experience of political fear. I was at the mercy of apparently unlimited power belonging to a person with his own ideas about what was good for me. The fear was sharpened by not understanding the rules, or understanding them but considering them silly. Which was irrelevant to the matter in hand – my role was to be frightened, and then to conform to the values of the powerful. Roald Dahl's local doctor had to persuade him to go back to his prep school after he feigned an illness to avoid another beating. 'Life is tough,' the doctor said, 'and the sooner you learn how to cope with it the better for you.'

We learned to cope. I have an early letter to my parents from Mr Walters, setting out the schedule of the term.

In the summer and autumn terms we have a half term leave out from the Friday morning early until Tuesday evening (6.00 p.m.): otherwise boys do not sleep out during term time. In addition, parents are welcome to take their son out twice on Sundays during term time (after the first three Sundays have elapsed and not on the last two Sundays of term). The boys are available from 11.00 a.m. (after chapel) and should return before 6.30 p.m.. You will also see your son on Parents' Days.

These longer terms lasted for twelve weeks or more, so apart from the five-day half-term, in three months a prep school boy might see his parents for a maximum of fifteen hours. And back in school uniform by 6.30 p.m. on Sunday, we'd be swallowing down tears to *The day Thou gavest Lord is ended (the darkness falls at Thy behest).*

Better get used to the total institution. I accepted the process of being re-socialised – the name, the clothes, the curtailment of self. Like Benedictine monks, we were continually changing dormitories or rooms so as not to become attached to any one place. This was in the guise of moving on, moving up. I absorbed myself into the collective identity. I ate the food on my plate. I didn't sing, whistle or put my hands in my pockets in the cloisters. I deferred to the teachers as Sir, and for the first days of the holidays said the same to my dad.

Even when not being beaten, plenty of smaller offences reminded us of the balance of power. Dirty hands at Inspection on the way into a meal, unpolished shoes, talking out of turn. Every form of perceived insolence was punished, usually by silence in the dining hall. We were condemned to a personal silence of five minutes, ten minutes or the whole meal. The entire school could be put on silence, which was almost unendurable because we weren't in the dining room to enjoy the food.

For what we are about to receive, may the Lord make us truly grateful.

After the clatter and scrape of a hundred chairs on a wooden floor, twelve-year-old boys (this was the age group entrusted with the jobs) provided table service to the school in a single sitting. The meals were plated in the kitchens and we picked them up at a hatch, two at a time, back and forth, hoping when the time came to claim a bigger or smaller portion (depending on what it was) as a reward for unpaid labour.

Three times a day the depth of our gratitude to the Lord was determined by access to fat and sugar, and as the same meals appeared in rotation our pleasure or regret was instant: we knew exactly what was coming. My favourite fat was in the soft yellow pastry on a stew of spongey meat, and in the deep-fried bread of the same glowing colour every breakfast. Once a week we had bought-in sausage rolls and beans, which meant desperate pleading with fate for a good one (soft, possibly undercooked) not a bad one (hard, burnt). For sugar, my favourite supply was custard on tinned red plums, and the pond of red jam in a crater of semolina. Some boys mixed the jam with the semolina to make a pink paste, which was insane and an abomination. On Saturday afternoons, after football matches, we had iced buns.

I remember the good stuff, the comfort where it could be found.

Cameron makes a point in his memoir of remembering a prep school meal of curry, rice and maggots. Presumably at Heatherdown this kind of treatment never did Prince Andrew any harm, and in any case private schools had long bumped up their profits by spending as little of the fee income as possible on catering. In the nineteenth century at Radley, hungry boys foraged for bulbs and cowslip roots.

By the 1970s these days of privation were nearly at an end. In the dormitories, the bedding changed from sheets and blankets (to be remade every morning, with hospital corners) to an amazing invention from Sweden or Switzerland called duvets. Never mind the details, feel the warmth. Change was coming, and a day boy called Charles – his surname – was allowed to bring in a Tupperware box containing his personal packed lunch. I have total recall of his skinny shoulders hunched over the plastic box as he picked through homely bits and pieces he wanted no one else to see. Presumably he had allergies. We mocked him, of course, and not only because he was a day boy and we boarders who suffered most were superior beings. Every day with his salad and his fresh fruit Charles betrayed the evidence of his mother's love. What a wet. What a crybaby. We were so jealous we made his life miserable.

The most accurate word for this spartan existence is austere. Every private school boy of my age has lived through a period of austerity. Never did me any harm, as the older generations like to say. For some, these were the best days of their lives, and the hardship is often justified as a preparation for life's inevitable darker turns. Stephen Fry credits his boarding school for allowing him to survive in prison, just as Evelyn Waugh suggested it would (though Waugh didn't test out his theory in person). The golf writer Henry Longhurst, a boy at St Cyprian's prep school with George Orwell, always protested that the school wasn't as tough as Orwell made out, yet he also relishes a letter from one of their contemporaries: 'it may amuse you to know that my brother attributes that he emerged absolutely sane and fit from five years as a prisoner of war solely to having been at St Cyprian's'.

If anyone deserved to survive, it was us. We were like cockroaches, tough-shelled and invincible, rubbish at expressions of joy but world-class at emotional and physical suffering, our bodies and our soft English hearts hardened at great expense. We were expected to endure, and to make endurance a habit.

Near the beginning, though, some natural intuition occasionally knew better. On a summer's evening in 1975, in my second term at boarding school, I was called out of my dormitory and taken along the corridor into the headmaster's side of the house. I was terrified. It was after the 8.15 frontier of 'lights out', but the evening was brimming with sunshine.

Goat Walters, in a tired but kindly way, sat me down in his living room and told me that my great-grandmother had died. In a book about the family written by my uncle I can check that her name was Alice Alfrida, born in 1885. She was ninety years old and I was eight. We lived in the same street but this was not a close relationship.

I was inconsolable. I went back to my bed and bawled my eyes out. I wept with abandon because I could: at last I had a reason that even the headmaster conceded was sad. My grief was out of all proportion to the event, but I was mourning the death of my lost life at home as it changed in my absence. I grieved without inhibition because I realised I couldn't go back – until then my great-grandmother had been part of my childhood, a small part but the home I'd known was disappearing without me. This rare but real outburst of emotion was already confused, self-protectively disguised.

An early lesson of these schools was sinking in: the importance of hiding genuine feeling, even from myself. Apart from that, I was fine.

4

Parents

'A friend of ours had to be heavily sedated in order to go to school. Perfectly normal chap now.'

Father of a boy at boarding school, *The Making of Them*, BBC *40 Minutes*, 1994

An enduring mystery of boarding schools, at least for the children, was why parents chose to make this decision. The experience was harrowing enough in 1975, but also in 1950 and 1930 and 1910. What was wrong with these people? Had they no heart?

In most cases, their education was to blame. The majority of fathers had suffered the same type of schooling themselves, so didn't know any better. Besides, it was worse in their day. Molesworth identifies the problem: 'the whole thing goes on and on and there is no stoping it it is a vicious circle.' The evidence is online in the school magazines, in the record of new arrivals to the various houses:

Salvete

Johnson's (A) 1984.3 P.L. Bristow (son of A.L. '54, grandson of R.L. '25)

Spens's (B) 1984.3 T.W. Ashwanden (son of D.N. '49, grandson of N.S.W '19)

Some families were trapped, as if in a cult. Generation after generation they continued with the existence they knew, even when they sensed it was wrong. In the 1994 documentary *The Making of Them*, when small boys are still being left aged eight in country houses with strangers, one of the well-to-do mums says, 'I am miserable about him going.' On the plus side, it's a 'lovely house'. She says 'it's not a drama' while affecting not to notice that in the car, in the echoing entrance hall, and again with his new friend he's only just met, her son is trying desperately not to cry.

The prep school in this film, Hawtreys near Marlborough in Wiltshire, closed down as a school later that year. But still in 1994 the dormitories had iron-framed beds I recognise and noisy wooden-floored corridors. For me this documentary is as compelling as a horror film. The bells! The bells! About halfway through I'm allowed inside the drawing room of one of the parents, a mum who's going to explain to me how she and her husband came to this decision. Her name is Caroline, and she sits on a faded pink sofa wearing a green blouse, with the flounced hair of the early nineties but the clipped voice of the private school ages. I quite like her – she's defending herself as if outnumbered. She explains that she's 'much happier without telephone contact' with her eight-year-old son. She knows of other boys who constantly ring their mothers to say 'please take me home'.

'They're not unhappy at all, but it's the obvious thing to say. It's rather obvious, really.'

Her eyes keep sliding to the left, as she remembers that her own brother ran away from his prep school. 'He didn't get very far. We never really got to the bottom of it.' Throughout the interview she's holding a silver fruit knife, and while speaking she turns it between her fingers then slips the point behind her wedding ring, as if wanting to cut it off.

What support she has comes from her husband, with his pastel-yellow jumper over a checked shirt and his side parting in flyaway hair. He has a different reason for not wanting to talk to his son on the phone. The standard of chat isn't up to much – eight-year-olds are 'very stilted' in their conversation. When the father tells the story of his friend from boarding school who had to be sedated, the interviewer sounds suitably astonished:

Father: I don't know what upset him about the place [laughs]. He used to be reduced to a state of coma, virtually, sort of dragged orf to school [laughs, wipes his eye].
Interviewer: Goodness.
Father: [wipes other eye, laughing] Pretty grim. [sniggers with an in-breath through his nose, wipes the first eye again] Pretty grim.

Interviewer: But it did him good in the end?
Father: [looks up at ceiling] Well, no, I think he hated it.
He should have probably stayed at home, or something.
[looks down]

In 1996, two-thirds of a survey of five thousand parents with children at boarding schools felt uncomfortable or guilty about splitting the family. Among these, some felt that sending children away to school was archaic and cruel. They did it anyway. For a small but influential tribe, an odd and unnatural idea had been normalised.

But normalisation doesn't help, in the long run. In the history of psychology, younger by far than the history of English private schools, the earliest clinical observations about former boarding school children were made in 1918 by the psychiatrist William Halse Rivers, famous for his treatment of soldiers suffering from shell shock. 'The public schoolboy enters the army with a long course of training behind him which enables him successfully to repress, not only the expression of fear, but also the emotion itself.'

In 1918, for understandable reasons, this wasn't unequivocally identified as a weakness, or even a problem. A hundred years later that conclusion is, however, being reached by an increasing number of mental health professionals. Leaders in the field include Joy Schaverien – notable for identifying 'Boarding School Syndrome', which describes the emotional trauma of early boarding – and Nick Duffell, who explores survival strategies adopted by adults he calls 'Boarding School Survivors'. These recent studies lean heavily on John Bowlby's twentieth-century research into attachment theory, and his emphasis on the importance of early emotional attachments in child development. Bowlby, who died in 1990, occasionally strayed from the scientific language befitting a Fellow of the Royal College of Physicians: 'I wouldn't send a dog away to boarding school aged seven.'

As yet, there is no formal quantitative research into psychological outcomes for ex-boarders, but Duffell persuasively argues that there isn't 'a single theory of child development that underpins or backs up the British practice of sending young children ... away from their families to reside in educational institutions for approximately seventy-five percent of each year'. Nevertheless, generations of parents know better than the experts: this, they decide, is for the best. They want what's best for their children.

In the case of my dad, he himself was a conflicted public school boy, neither fully in nor out. During the war his older brother had been sent to board in Devon, and seven years later my father took the same journey, waved off on the train with a pre-written card to put in the post to say he'd arrived. Both sons left school at seventeen and back in Swindon set to growing the family building business. Two generations earlier, in 1911, the company founder's own father had died alone and drunk in the Reading workhouse, so it's fair to speculate that the family was testing out boarding schools as an accelerated class-laundering scheme. Dad must have concluded, when his turn came as a parent, that with more ambition we'd be able to wash whiter. He lived half a mile from his parents in his home town, doing the same job his dad did. In terms of social mobility he had unfinished business, and the post-war building boom had brought in the money. By spending a bit bigger he'd save me from the fate that was his.

In *The Old Boys*, a historical survey of public schools, David Turner explains that a regular feature of this form of education, right from the start, was 'of preventing downward social mobility, rather than encouraging upward social mobility'. The traditional customer base had plenty of money and they wanted more money, or in the next generation to keep what money they had. My dad, like his own dad before him, was pushing in the opposite direction. For a while, through the sixties and seventies, Swindon was the fastest growing town in Europe, and an obvious benefit to the family of Swindon's prosperity was the financial clout to avoid Swindon's local schools and eventually, if all went well, the town of Swindon itself. Dad's private school escape strategy wasn't cheap, but he could almost afford it.

He treated school fees like a tax, payable against access to the better professions and people and places of the United Kingdom. With this in mind, the stately home settings made a lot of sense: the schools didn't look like our semi-detached house in Swindon, but like a country pile in the dreams of a socially ambitious provincial builder. On the internet I google images for Heatherdown, Cameron's prep school. Demolished in 1989, the main red-brick building was ten windows long and three windows high, set in thirty acres of grounds. Johnson's Ashdown House was built in the eighteenth century and designed by the same architect responsible for the front portico of the White

House. According to the school's website, Ashdown is 'blessed with magnificent and extensive grounds'. These are the playing fields in which to plant boys who will grow into successful Englishmen.

To be fair to my dad, he did show some half-heartedness about sending his children away. Although I boarded from the age of eight and two days, Pinewood was a twenty-minute drive from Old Town Swindon. Radley was an hour away along the A420 past Faringdon. Somewhere inside himself Dad had an instinct that was almost natural: he wanted his sons close to home.

Our points of contact were match days. Dad's silent touchline vigil at the rugby and the football and the hockey, or on his chair beyond the boundary at cricket, replaced the full-time connection we didn't have. He used to skip work to watch the matches against other schools and usually Mum would turn up too, arriving separately from home, and she'd bring a cake. In the list of sub-stitutes for affection, as recorded in my careful Sunday letters, I ask at different times for sweet chestnuts, Kendal Mint Cake, a hairbrush and dressing gown, a game, some pencils, some books, golf tees and a golf ball, sweeties and *my flannel and my shoe-cleaning kit, which is under the bed.* God knows how we'd have managed if I hadn't made the teams.

Dad had good reason to make this decision with half a heart: himself a product of boarding school, he was uncomfortable with emotional engagement and haunted by a lost sense of self. He was drinking too much. This began to make itself evident during the holiday evenings at home, where he sat apart from the television with a cigar and a refillable tumbler of Teacher's whisky and one of his many books by or about Winston Churchill. He'd have known that Churchill, in his own words, 'was to go away from home for many weeks at a stretch in order to do lessons under masters', and that at boarding school fabulous Winston was ferociously beaten.

It worked out well enough for Churchill, and at the height of his Churchill phase Dad must have hoped it would work out well for me. With the right start in life, I could become prime minister, an idea that up until about the general election of 2010 I found utterly ridiculous. My dad was out of touch. Privately educated boys from boarding schools in the Home Counties would never be prime minister again: the electorate had found these people out.

Though apparently not. The great British public didn't have the information to know for sure what we were like, those of us educated in this specific period in these particular schools. Nor did my dad. He assumed my education would be better than his: he was paying more money than his own father had, and the world had moved on. Except in many significant ways it hadn't.

There were warnings, as there always have been, but he ignored them. The school fees tax, like it or not, also contributes towards qualifying as a published writer, and over the years public school authors have been consistent heretics: these schools get battered by anyone with a pen and a capacity for independent thought. The tradition of boarding school dissidents connects Graves to Galsworthy and Maugham to Trollope, with many illustrious stations in between, from the historian Gibbon to the philosopher John Locke. Another historian, little Thomas Macaulay, only escaped because a sympathetic adult wrote to his mother that 'throwing boys headlong into those great public schools always puts me in mind of the practice of the Scythian mothers, who threw their new-born infants into the river'.

C. S. Lewis, famous for his warm and open Narnian heart, wrote a memoir called *Surprised By Joy: The Shape of My Early Life*. He calls his first boarding school 'Belsen', evidently from the period of his early life before joy surprised him. Graham Greene was no more of an enthusiast, nor Bertrand Russell nor L. P. Hartley. Writers have opposed Britain's private school system for the same reason Orwell claimed that writers fought the Spanish Falangists: as authors they had the free time. Which didn't make them wrong, in either case.

Even in politics, the occasional prime minister shuddered at the memories. William Pitt the Elder thought that 'a public school might suit a boy of turbulent disposition but would not do where there was any gentleness'. He educated Pitt the Younger at home and young William prime-ministered at the age of twenty-four. Clearly, the lack of a boarding school education didn't hold him back, not that ambitious parents took much notice. The point to make here is that in 1975, when choosing a school for their children, the parents had no excuse for not knowing the challenges their children were likely to face. They always knew.

And yet. A boarding school education remained a desirable commodity, and parents paid handsomely for the privilege. Pinewood had a main building that dated from 1845, nine windows long and three high, with eighty-four acres of grounds and classrooms in the old stables and coach houses. The 1975 prospectus promised to 'guide the boys through their critical early years of development', obviously not a job to entrust to parents. The Pinewood boy would 'develop a good competitive spirit', and the school 'will encourage a Christian attitude to life – not something just for Sundays'. And of course the preparatory school prepared the boy to pass the Common Entrance exam that enabled entrance to a respectable public school. In the prospectus Eton is mentioned by name.

As is Plato, in the section *From the Headmaster*, who 'tells us that the development of character is more important than the acquisition of knowledge'. In fact, come the twenty-first century, in a turn of events the headmaster was unlikely ever to have imagined, a 'character' could prosper with very little knowledge at all. 'We do look for enthusiasm.' The other big sell is the range of facilities, which then as now have a dogfood factor. The photograph of the fully equipped 1970s science lab is to persuade the buyer, not the consumer. And for some parents and children, the same will be true of the games pitches. In tone, the prospectus reflects the timeless quality of the period, promising results not dissimilar to those in the report of the 1861 Clarendon Commission, established to investigate complaints about the nine leading schools in England at that time:

> It is not easy to estimate the degree to which the English people are indebted to these schools for ... [giving boys]

74

their capacity to govern others and control themselves, their aptitude for combining freedom with order, their public spirit, their vigour and manliness of character, their strong but not slavish respect for public opinion, their love of healthy sports and exercise. These schools have been the chief nurseries of our statesmen.

A hundred years after Clarendon, Erving Goffman recognises that a total institution should be 'viewed as a place for generating assumptions about identity'. I take this to mean that in our enclosed world we could refine a collective delusion about who we were, or who we ought to want to be. Or as Radley Warden Dennis Silk warns a daunted audience of new boys in *Public School*, we were expected to pick up 'the right habits for life'.

Among these habits was cultivation of the stiff upper lip. We could be ourselves – homesick, vulnerable, lovelorn and frightened – or, with practice at putting up a front, we could embody the idealised national character. We could learn to be loyal and robust and self-reliant. Wearing a commendably brave face we could distance our feelings and do without, growing the 'hardness of heart of the educated' identified by Mahatma Gandhi. He meant the privately educated English ruling class he'd encountered in South Africa and India. We needed to be stoical and busy if we aspired to the full catastrophe of the English gentleman, whose dividend for shutting down emotions was invincibility at times of stress, such as quelling an uprising on the North-West Frontier. This psychological disaster was celebrated in the boarding schools as a desirable national outcome. The English didn't fall apart. Look at the history books and see how productive this quality could be.

After the long-haired shock of the sixties, no parent with conservative tendencies wanted a spoiled child. The antidote was the austere upbringing that had produced solid Empire children since the glory days of Charles Dickens. Except the parents, too, had been influenced by 1968 – couldn't the nine-year-old Olivers please have some more? On the Pinewood School bill for 1976, the Matron's Account includes entries for a term's worth of Extra Fruit (£2.25) along with Extra Milk (£1.89), which meant *some* fruit and *some* milk, an orange or apple a day, and half a pint of milk in a blue Bakelite mug. The times they were a-changing, but because boarding schools were deliberately set apart from the main social flow, more slowly here than anywhere else.

The parents, rattling around at home in huge empty houses, believed they were doing what was best for their children. If challenged at a drinks party (and at the right drinks parties, they seldom were) do say: we value the teacher–pupil ratio, the discipline and the range of activities the school has to offer. The facilities are first-rate. Don't say: I'm in favour of entrenched inequality and limiting the opportunities for British children whose parents don't have the money. Do say: I have nothing to be ashamed of, I'm prepared to make sacrifices (but don't add – for the sake of social advancement). Do say: he seems so happy there, he's making lots of new friends. Don't say: the end justifies the means, and one day, God willing, you'll be looking at the proud mum and dad of one of the most important people in the country. If not *the* most important. Stranger things have happened.

In return for the abandonment and institutionalisation of their child, the parents gained status and adult liberation from the daily constraints of 'not in front of the children'. They outsourced the unkind England of *I want never gets* and *spare the rod spoil the child*, paying for a culture of intolerance they didn't have the heart or the time to enforce at home. 'Our daily enemies remain sloppiness, selfishness and self-indulgence,' writes the Warden in 1983, so two-thirds of his attack was always aimed at the self. 'They always were and they always will be. So long as we all remain clear about this we will have a chance of success.'

The objective of boarding school was to make us intolerant of sloppiness, imprecision, unpunctuality, grammatical error, litter, graffiti and also of our own selves if we stepped out of line. Whereas boys deprived of this education were spoiled. They were selfish and self-indulgent. If, even so, they were loved, we were as intolerant of this weakness as any other. We had high standards, designed to act as a shield and a safety net, protecting us from misfortune and failure. Our parents were investing money in making us future-proof. Whether we received 'the best education available' always remained debatable, but for those prices it certainly should have been the safest, not just for conventional life chances but physically, keeping commonplace dangers at bay.

I was first drunk at the age of eleven, while celebrating the burning of Catholics. Every year on Bonfire Night the school allowed a carnival-type ritual where boys in groups of four or five took charge of a rusty metal barrel with holes punched in the lower third. In the woods after dark we built fires inside the barrels and cooked sausages in pans on the flames. In our wellington boots and blue boiler suits we drank fizzy drinks from the bottle and larked about. One year my group went to the village shop, but instead of cherryade or orangeade or lemonade, we bought appleade. It was Woodpecker cider, and that night I stumbled and fell, blind drunk, between the lit open fires of other small boys in baggy blue overalls and wellingtons. That wasn't very health and safety (and 'appleade' was the story we told the headmaster. We knew cider was naughty, but we had no idea how good it was at doing what it did, or how quick. The TV adverts didn't mention the vomiting or the retching or the raddled canopy of November leaves spinning in the smoke from the fires).

At one stage a haemophiliac arrived at the school whose name I remember as Ashley. Perhaps, because of his illness, he was permitted a first name. A haemophiliac! At a 1970s boys' boarding school! That wasn't going to turn out well, and it didn't. You couldn't be a boy at this school at this time in the twentieth century and not bleed. I remember – and every time I say I remember, without documentary evidence I might be wrong – an incident near the cricket nets and a ball to the teeth. He left soon after.

Nevertheless, for the parents a private boarding school was a supposedly safe bet. The odds were in our favour, if not immediately then for success in the future, and mums and dads across the country were prepared to wager on paid strangers raising their son as 'a broadly based all-rounder', qualifying him for membership of a club comprising 'good chaps who knew how to play the game'. Dad wanted the benefits as advertised in the prospectus – 'development of character', 'good results' – because the process was so unquestionably effective. He heard private education in the pinched accents of Cabinet ministers on the nine o'clock news, in the updates of generals from the Falklands, in the Christmas dinner address of the president of the local Conservative club. England's top people had been educated together for a very long time, from the fourteenth century onwards, with the aim by the Victorian period of cosying up close to the Upper Ten Thousand, as the elite then liked to call themselves.

School fees in return for preferment. By the laws of the free market, which Mrs Thatcher at about this time started to push as her own chosen theory of human nature, people paid because it worked. The parents were making a prudent investment.

As for becoming prime minister – if this destination was implicitly achievable at every imitation Eton, at Eton itself the pathway was signposted in weatherproof paint. Twenty prime ministers have been Old Etonians, a quarter of them since the Second World War. The debt they owe to their schooling is often explicit and unashamed: Lord Rosebery (prime minister 1894–95) had the Eton Boating Song played at his funeral. Lord Curzon, not quite PM but Viceroy of India from 1899 to 1905 and later Foreign Secretary, kept a room at his home Kedleston Hall as an exact replica of his boyhood room at Eton. Even so, in his diaries Sir Henry 'Chips' Channon describes Curzon as 'less Eton-orientated than many of his generation'.

In 1975 the upper and ridiculous limit of eighteen Etonian prime ministers seemed to have been reached. Eton's elitist, restrictive style of education was old and tired, yet at the price of many decimal pounds and the stiff-lipped separation of families, the gears of social advancement continued to turn: these schools kept up their manufacture of jacketed and tied pseudo-adults, loyal to a specific class and culture, impervious to social progress. Family routines were replaced by tribal rituals and beatings and a school language impenetrable to outsiders, but then we had little time for outsiders. Isolated, powerless, young children were hazed into the ruling class in a Faustian pact that offered worldly success at the cost of emotional damage.

The success hides the damage. Joy Schaverien realised early in her research into Boarding School Syndrome that in England there was a 'cultural taboo' against noticing the problem of deliberately fractured family attachments. If we ended up with the best jobs, why fix the education that served us so well? The damage was socially condoned by a high-status tribe that among other failings had a reluctance to admit being wrong. The godfather of attachment theory, John Bowlby, called public school 'the traditional first step in the time-honoured barbarism required to produce English gentlemen'. It's a problem for those who go through it, but also for everyone else: the damage trickles down, like a mockery of the theory of wealth creation so beloved of Conservatives. These people, my people, are in charge – the country as a whole should expect to share the pain.

Dad did sometimes wonder if it was worth the money. I have a reply from the Radley bursar to a letter of his dated 6 May 1980, acknowledging his payment of my first term's fees. Dad must have questioned the linen hire charge for sheets and pillowcases (including laundry), even though (or perhaps because) a form of social laundering was what he was paying for. And pay he must: '... this is a once-for-all charge made on the first account to cover the loan of linen throughout his time with us. This is found to be a fairer arrangement to parents than getting them to supply these items and avoids identity problems arising.'

The parents signed the pact – we the children did what we were told, isolating for the long haul despite the arising identity problems. A common mitigation of high-achieving privately schooled adults is that they didn't choose their education. While this is true, they often choose it again, when the time comes with their own children. On and on it goes, just as Molesworth pointed out in 1957, a vicious circle unbroken because whatever the individual hardships in 1975, the social and professional benefits would be felt in the future. As Hannah Arendt says in *The Origins of Totalitarianism*, 'there is hardly a better way to avoid discussion than by releasing an argument from the control of the present and by saying that only the future can reveal its merits'. It was for our own good, just wait and see.

Hannah Arendt is my second elective guardian, the educator along with Erving Goffman I'd have chosen if I'd had the choice. Arendt was born in Hanover in 1906, and in 1933 was denounced by the Nazi Party for her research into anti-Semitic propaganda. She was imprisoned by the Gestapo before fleeing to France, and from there to the United States, where she settled in New York and became an American citizen in 1950. She died in 1975. I don't know where she ranked in her class of political philosophers, but she did have the wisdom to escape her affair with Martin Heidegger when she was his student at the University of Marburg. Heidegger aspired to being the official philosopher to the Nazis, and included information about his affairs in his letters to his wife.

The photograph I like best of Hannah Arendt is from her early forties, where she's leaning over a table, weight on her elbows and cigarette in hand, wearing a dark shirt with at the throat a silver brooch fastening the pointed collars. Her short hair is unruly, even more so in the shadow on the wall behind her, and her intelligent eyes are weary from reading everything. She is fully engaged in listening, and prepared to question every word I say.

5

Separation

'J. M. H. Lovegrove is one of this term's crop of stigs, or new boys. He's about to take up residence in his new home, C Social ... for the next five years, he will spend more time in this house than his own home.'

Richard Denton, voiceover, *Public School*, BBC
Television, 1980

Through close contact with others in the same situation, parents immunised themselves to criticism of boys' boarding schools. They developed herd immunity, pretending not to know that at the expense of poorer British children their sons would later have the pick of the country's choicest opportunities. There was an obvious response to this injustice, in the Thatcherite spirit of the

1980s that was gradually taking hold: so what? We paid for it.

In a Faustian pact, at some stage someone is going to get hurt. At night the little men in ties and jackets reverted to little children in name-taped pyjamas with a single soft toy (also name-taped) blubbing themselves to sleep and wetting their beds. This physical discomfort – the cold, the food – was the surface experience. Even the beating was a short sharp shock, as promoted by the British Navy, because physical punishment didn't waste time or use up resources. It was cheap, quick and over when it was over. Everyone could move on. Whereas the administrative inconvenience of other punishments, apparently, risked making the miscreant feel important.

The deeper, emotional austerity started from the moment the parents drove away.

Goffman pays close attention to the psychological impact of the handover, when individuals enter total institutions for the first time. Often, the reassurances given in advance are open to question: 'you'll have such fun', 'it's for your own good', 'we want the best for you'. The responsible adults equivocate, parents and teachers alike, and with luck a young child will not have to 'look directly at what is happening or to deal with the raw emotion that his situation might well cause him to express'. In retrospect, Goffman concludes, 'a new patient may feel that everyone's comfort was being busily sustained while his long-range welfare was being undermined'.

My own greatest fear was that my parents would leave before I'd said goodbye. We were often in different places during the handover – the boys upstairs for housekeeping in the dormitories, perhaps the parents in the headmaster's office for adult chat about money or verrucas. I was frightened that once we were apart my parents would leave and either they or I would die and I wouldn't have said goodbye. The word had to be said. Goodbye. Not much point in saying see you soon, but maybe we lied about that, too.

In the first episode of *Public School*, as the cars drive away, Richard Denton, the director and narrator, makes sure the viewer understands exactly what's happening: 'Left alone ... ' he says, over a shot of a small boy in a dormitory. There are still nine episodes to go, but being left alone was the main thing, and everything that followed was a reaction to that. I remember crying, and being desperate to hide the crying, but the details of where I hid and how long it lasted are lost in the amnesia. The feeling of desolate homesickness, however, can be reignited by Colin Luke's brilliant documentary *The Making of Them*, about eight-year-old boys navigating their first days at Hawtreys. This school was one of Pinewood's rivals at cricket and rugby, and the boys there had to cope with their own loud staircases and oversized windows.

In the film a brave-faced small boy confesses that 'Bagnall caught me crying'. Then he corrects the word 'caught' to 'found'. Bagnall found him crying, but honestly nothing was wrong with that. The camera focuses on another small boy hiding his face against a pillar to take off his glasses and wipe away tears. He is quickly surrounded by older boys.

'Are you homesick?'

'No.'

Abruptly, several times a year, our attachments to home and family were broken. We lost everything – parents, pets, toys, younger siblings – and we could cry if we liked but no one would help us. So that later in life, when we saw other people cry, we felt no great need to go to their aid. The sad and the weak were wrong to show their distress, and projecting our misery onto others we learned to despise the children who blubbed for their mummies. Go on, blub your eyes out, but it won't change anything: life doesn't work like that. At school the cure was to stop crying and forget that life beyond the dormitories and classrooms existed. Concentrate instead on the games' pitches and the dining hall and the headmaster's study. By force of will we made ourselves complicit in a collective narrowing of vision.

This wasn't healthy, and it wasn't just me. Joy Schaverien's Boarding School Syndrome is now a condition sufficiently recognised to merit therapy groups and an emergent academic literature in the *British Journal of Psychotherapy*. The symptoms are wide-ranging but include, engrained from an early age, emotional detachment and dissociation, cynicism, exceptionalism, defensive arrogance, offensive arrogance, cliquism, compartmentalisation, guilt, grief, denial, strategic emotional misdirection and stiff-lipped stoicism. Fine fine fine. I'm fine.

We adapted to survive. Abandoned, alone, England's future leaders needed to fit in whatever the cost. As for love and forgiveness, the exceptionalist English schoolboy convinced himself early that he had no great need of either. He was not needy, no sir, and could live without. He went to chapel twice a day and learned that God was his shepherd and he shall not want. Those were the words, whatever they meant. He did not want. He prayed himself to sleep in his dormitory and woke in fear of weakness, of revealing himself as wet or girly or a crybaby. The teachers preferred the terms 'pathetic' or 'childish'. 'Grow up, boy!' Being a grown-up meant needing no one.

Terrified of crying for help, of complaining or sneaking, we developed a gangster loyalty to self-contained cliques, scared to death of being cast out, of being cast out again, as we had been from home. In the absence of family we kept in with our chums, but also ingratiated ourselves with the teachers: God knows what came next after abandonment if we kicked up a fuss.

Much later, in certain circles, the label 'Remoaner' would resonate with disproportionate force. As a taunt, it was the brainchild of the privately educated, a bully word fashioned by those who understood this system and anyone influenced by it. A complainer was the worst thing a boarder could be. 'Nobody ever complained,' the poet Andrew Motion writes in his memoir *In the Blood*, 'because nobody ever listened. Not even our Mums and Dads.' A moaner, a blubber, a crybaby. Worse, a *re*moaner – a recidivist, someone who moaned again and again, who at the start of every new term failed to understand the rules of English belonging. Anyone that pathetic deserved to be ridiculed.

This was perfectly normal. For showing vulnerability, the remoaners and the weak would be scapegoated in a tradition going back to the Middle Ages, when every form at Eton had an official dunce. The *custos* was the weakest boy in the class, singled out for goading until he could pretend to be stronger, at which point the unwanted title passed to someone else. Instinctively, we knew to look around for the *custos*. If you couldn't identify him, it was you. It wasn't me, it was the boy Charles with his plastic lunch box. In 1976 it was Hardcastle who wore glasses, and who in the first few terms was my friend. By the second year, if he as much as brushed against me, I had to wipe the stain from my sweater to free myself for higher-tariff friendships involving popularity and power.

We played endless games of It, a dodging and weaving game, where one person is contaminated while the others run free, all while regulating our boy hierarchies with finely calibrated banter. From the teachers we learned about mockery and sarcasm as techniques for social control, and banter could range from a sharp remark to a knuckle in the crown of the head. Attack was the best form of defence, and ridicule was honed as a deeply conservative force, controlling by means of fear, either of being the joke or of not getting the joke. There was plenty of fear to go round. Paul Watkins remembers at Eton the huge amount of energy, in the time of Cameron and Johnson, that went into 'teasing and ignoring people'. 'I felt a coldness and a harshness that I'd never felt before.'

To hide our fear and other vulnerabilities, we learned not to be easily impressed. Wary of pranks and straightforward lies, designed to humiliate the victim, we assumed that everything was a racket until proven otherwise. We saw something beautiful and called it 'ridiculous'. Any boy, but especially a friend, could be laughed out of a dubious pursuit that risked diminishing the status of the group. Orwell remembers being ridiculed out of his interest in butterflies. The banter that day must have been immense. Nothing was sacred, and once we found out what another boy took most seriously we were ready to strike, when necessary, at its core. Our most effective defence was therefore to act as if we took nothing very seriously at all.

We learned to stay detached, some would say cold – 'You had to have a coldness in yourself,' writes Watkins. 'Of all the rules I learned and later threw away, this one I kept. If you did not know it, you could get hurt very badly at a place like Eton.' These schools nurtured the hurt and the hurters, and most boys at some time were both. In self-defence we discovered the ice-walls of irony, an opaque distancing mechanism that didn't let anyone or anything come too close. In the school magazines from this period the teenage writers specialise in irony, striking this or that pose without admitting to genuine pleasure or pain or in fact any discernibly strong feeling at all. 'Not bad,' we said, when we liked something. Every emotional storm was contained, to our own satisfaction, in a teacup. The smallness of the cup was made more of a priority than the storm.

Our parents had duped us once, telling us about the fun we'd have and by leaving us here in the first place: we wouldn't be fooled again. Solid British common sense meant cynicism – in our bleak view of life cynicism was healthy because, well, it was common sense. Even a mother's love was a trick, lasting only until the beginning of each new term, and cynicism was preferable to despair, which we were as likely to admit to feeling as we were to our yearning for love. Don't be soft, boy, betraying the soft influence of home, which needed to be quickly swapped out for the hard pragmatism of school. We got used to it, and no aspect of boarding school life demonstrates this shift as clearly as the weekly letters home.

In this form, at least, I write like George Orwell, more than sixty years earlier. Prep school had changed so little that our letters echo each other across the century. Here's sad George encoding his cry for help in 1911:

My dear Mother,
    I hope you are quite well. I am top in arithmetic, and I have been moved up in Latin.

Here's sad Richard, in about 1977:

Dear Mummy and Daddy,
    I hope you are well. I scored 32 not out and got 3 catches in an 'A' eleven match against St Hughes 1st XI. I opened the batting.

My dear Mother, [writes George]
    What kind of weather are you having? We are having lots of rain, but it is not raining this morning. But it is very dull. Will you please send me one or two of the new penny stamps for I have not got one yet.

Dear Mummy and Daddy,

Has it been snowing in Swindon? It is very cold at school and has been snowing. Please will you send my penknife?

Our letters have the common theme of reassurance through boasting (it's all right! I'm doing well so the broken-up family is worth it! Really!), neediness (please will you send penknives and shoe-brushing kits and penny stamps and the result of the FA Cup final?) and thanks (for the letter, for taking me out on Sunday). The gratitude ends up sounding like a repeat of the need. Orwell's biographer Bernard Crick has a blind spot here: 'There is no evidence of disturbance in these letters … a child in terror would write more briefly and in safe and easy stock phrases.' Orwell's phrases are so stock and safe they crop up almost identically over sixty years later, and can be parodied by Molesworth:

Dearest Mummy (and Daddy)
We played against porridge court on Saturday. We lost 9–0.
The film was a western. Will you send me a bakterial gun.
They are 6/6 at grabbers.
With love from
Nigel

That bracketed Daddy is impeccable – above all, whatever else these letters said, we wanted our mummies but could never express that ache directly. *Dear Mummy and Daddy, Thankyou very much for coming to Abingdon to watch us play rugby, I hope you enjoyed it. In case you did not know, we won 11–0.* They were there, on the sidelines, but it was as if they couldn't see what was in front of their eyes. As usual, the reliable Goffman has an explanation: 'It is a melancholy human fact that after a time all three parties – inmate, visitor, and staff – realize that the visiting room presents a dressed-up view, realise that the other parties realise this, too, and yet all tacitly agree to continue the fiction.'

We must have done something terribly wrong to be sent away from home in the first place, and we couldn't afford to compound that error now. We needed to ingratiate, to hold whatever we had. *I hope you liked having me on Sunday.* Ingratiation was another skill at which we learned to excel.

The letters home were important, but apart from mentions of Dutch elm disease and flu injections and breakfast by candlelight during power cuts, re-reading these letters now provides a limited informational haul. Molesworth is on hand to explain why: 'In fact, let us face it, boys do not like wrting home chiz and for a joly good reason. *There is nothing to sa.* Why? Because the truth is so shoking and unspekable that no parent could stand it on a Monday morning.'

And the truth is that we're living weeks on end without love, and when the pitches are waterlogged we're running cross-country and sockless through driving rain over dark-ploughed January fields. Boys are weeping and shoes are submerged and lost, bone-chilled stragglers stumbling back to the big house barefoot in the fade of afternoon light, hindsight-trained as World War I first lieutenants, miserable and doomed. I didn't know how to write that in a letter home. It was too much to contemplate. I was eight.

Mum's letters in the other direction were equally careful. She didn't want to make us sad.

Daddy and I went to the cinema yesterday we saw James Bond, in 'The Man with the Golden Gun' we did enjoy it! It was very silly! There were a lot of car chases with cars doing somersaults, and skidding in circles! and one even turned into an aeroplane, and flew away!!!

She tried so hard, and the breathless exclamation marks of her child-free life were horrendously cheerful, or would have been if we'd believed in their excitement. Even a small boy could sense that extreme punctuation was fancy dress, and not real, and so in itself another cause for sadness. If none of us were enjoying this, why were we doing it? Instead of asking that question, we practised emotional evasion from Sunday last through to Sunday next. *Dear Mummy and Daddy, Thankyou for my nice holiday. I like it at Pinewood. It is very nice here. I am running out of sweeties, could you send some more?*

That was how it began in my first letter home dated 18 January 1975. Less than a week in and already running low on comfort food. In my case, this unfolding sequence of evasion and lies was occasionally broken by rogue grandparents, estranged from my mum who they no doubt felt was getting above herself socially. From a distance my grandma liked to stir the pot: *I know Mummy misses you.*

Three years later, by 1978 and aged eleven, I could block out this kind of truth, meaning the letters descend into agonising cruelty. To reassure my mum, I tell her I'm not missing a thing. *Thank you very much for your letter. I did not expect it so early in the term. School is great and much less boring than at home.*

Or as Molesworth says: 'Note the cooling of the ardour. O woe agane but that is the tragedy.'

What the letters hide so aggressively, especially *so early in the term*, is the homesickness, which as a feeling was like loneliness in its most concentrated form. Our inner selves were sick with fear and grief and loss, and the only cure was going back home. If that wasn't going to happen (it wasn't) the feelings needed to be shoved out of sight, which was made easier by the insane busy-ness of an average boarding school day. The outer uniformed self jumped at the bells and was exuberantly active from the beginning of this to the end of that, as advertised in the prospectus:

7.15 Everyone rises and makes his own bed
7.45 Breakfast (cereal, eggs, bacon or fish, bread, butter and marmalade, tea)
8.05 Inspection
8.10 Surgery
8.20 A brisk run down the drive for some fresh air
8.35 Morning prayers in the chapel

And so on, each day an epic of character-building in increments of under an hour, and it was still only half past eight. We needed to be kept occupied, with little respite from enthusiasm, because the worst response was to stand still and feel: what was lost could not be recovered. *We enjoyed having you home on your Sunday out, and we're already looking forward to your next Sunday!* Despite Mum's attempts to string hope from one exeat outing to the next, it didn't usually feel as if I'd soon be home. This was false information, and adults couldn't be trusted. Economists, surgeons, lawyers, politicians: whatever their field of expertise, for hundreds of years the top professionals in Britain have lied to their children. They don't have the first idea of what's for the best.

'Boarding schools and slums produce many of the same emotional outcomes,' says David Turner in *The Old Boys*, a book broadly in favour of private schools. For Turner, a former education correspondent of *The Times*, as well as for many others, the suppression of feelings for the sake of personal advancement is a price worth paying. Denial was how we survived, belittling our emotional experiences, like, for example, homesickness or the vacuum of love that thinned the dormitory air. We were encouraged to disbelieve in what we were feeling, and therefore gradually in any inner emotional core – what brains we had were used to depersonalise our selves and put our emotions into compartments. This was not an optimal psychological outcome, not for England's leaders, not for anyone.

Unless, of course, remoteness was a virtue, invaluable in a crisis. Another old-fashioned attribute, while detaching ourselves as thoroughly as possible, was our lack of attachment to material objects. We certainly knew not to bring anything to school that was precious to us, so that later in life we didn't make the mistake of caring too much about a sofa stained with spilt red wine, for example, especially if it belonged to someone else. Don't make a fuss about nothing, and by refusing to fuss we turned the concerns of others into nothing. Everything could be nothing, up could be down, right could be wrong. The truth could be a lie and one thing could always be another. *I like it at Pinewood. It is very nice here.* Our lies were generally well received, and to quote another expert (poets are supposed to be expertly sensitive) Andrew Motion decided that his 'best way to deal with school was to say all kinds of things I didn't mean, but people wanted to hear, until they joined up and became like a kind of skin'.

After Pinewood the Sunday letter-writing stopped being compulsory, and my correspondence from Radley pares down to requests, either for permissions or for food. I wrote home at the end of the first week, out of habit, and my letter is aware of the function it ought to fulfil. *It's great fun here. I am a bit miserable about my arm.* Just my arm, mind, which had been broken a week before in a game of garden football. That honestly-not-a-lot-miserable letter home ends with a *PS*.

Then a *PPS*.

And a *PPPS*.

And a *PPPPS*.

I desperately didn't want to say goodbye, but indirectly, not so anyone would notice until forty years later. I was being ironic. I was joking.

The emotional content was clumsily hidden, for my own protection. Nick Duffell, a pioneer in this therapeutic field, argues that strategies such as these demonstrate a survival personality common among early boarders. However confident we may appear, as children or adults, our fragile inner world needs protecting with constant vigilance. Other people can't be trusted – not the parents, definitely not the other boys – and in any case we have to hide our essential badness and unlovability.

Duffell takes the trouble to talk us through this predicament in Colin Luke's film *The Making of Them*, and on-screen in 1994 Duffell is softly spoken, bearded, about forty-five years old. He's wearing a tie, but over a soft-collared shirt with the top button undone. His glasses hang round his neck on a string. He looks like a leftie, like a wet, but seeing me for what I am he speaks slowly to camera as if to a child. He role-plays on my behalf, in the hope I'll lower my defences and listen to what he's explaining is wrong with me:

'Mummy and Daddy say they love me.' (Possibly, Nick, but in those days not even the saying of the words was a certainty.)

'If they love me, why did they send me away?' (A question worth asking, I agree.)

'It's important to them, and cost them a lot of money, so don't disappoint them by saying "I don't like it".' (I didn't. I never said that!)

'Then they won't love me.' (That was the risk, undeniably.)

'If I don't like it, something is wrong with me. That's why they sent me away.'

It's a trap, a classic double-bind – either my parents don't love me and sent me away because there's something wrong with me (not good for future self-esteem) or they do love me, and now if I feel they don't I must have something wrong with me (ditto). One way to counter and deny this compounded sense of failure was to bury the dilemma beneath a mound of success. At school everything was a competition, especially in the classroom. Like prisoners, when we weren't being beaten we were being questioned, on Latin vocabulary, the leadership qualities of Macbeth, the structure of the Artesian well. If we didn't have the answer we'd be punished, but mostly we responded eagerly with a craving for validation. We wanted to be told we were good, like dogs. Good boy. Who's a good boy? You are.

We competed to be top of the class as if winning would make us more lovable, as if praise could be a substitute for the love we lived without. We learned that life was a contest for approval, and every second letter home ended with an obligatory progress report. *Here are my first/ second/third fortnightly order marks.* The subjects then follow with a percentage and a class position for each, and the final summing up: *I came 11th out of a class of twenty boys.*

In my letters home I often mention I'm doing well and my mum replies *yes, well done for doing well.* No, really. *My best lesson is tests.* In my dad's rare letters he always has some variation on *well done* and *I hope you do well,* usually both, the jagged black spikes of his terrible handwriting full of conviction and psychic disorder. *I can't read*

Daddy's writing. 'Perfectly legible,' he'd say, except for the time when he was in hospital expecting to die from cancer and wrote from his bed in capital letters. I AM SURE YOU WILL DO VERY WELL. He was no more open to his feelings than I was.

Doing well fulfilled the pragmatic aspects of the transaction. One day I'd be prime minister (if I had high enough marks), and then the fear and the denial and the social brutality would have been worth whatever they cost.

Alas, these adjustments gestated a new kind of fear: the fear of failure. In his memoir *Flannelled Fool: A Slice of Life in the Thirties*, the journalist T. C. Worsley 'wasn't frightened of punishment' – he'd mastered the hard exterior – 'I was frightened of being drowned in a deep pool of inability, from which I would never be able to climb out'. *Never.* For boys exiled at school, the stakes of the fortnightly form order couldn't be higher. No words of comfort or explanation could be shared that evening at home, or any other evening, and my position in a class of nine or fifteen or twenty boys was my communication that I was surviving. Honestly. *I came first out of a class of fifteen boys.*

Hide your feelings, do as well as you can, and before long believe in no other life but this. We were very much in favour of being in control – '✔ ✘ ✔ ✘ ✔, thank you, sir' – because a loosening of the grip was dangerously close to falling apart. It's no accident that James Joyce sees Robinson Crusoe as the 'true prototype' of this version of Englishness. Abandoned, lonely, emotions in check, Crusoe seeks to control his desert island self without outside help. And when he does get help, he neglects to credit Man Friday for his contribution. Joyce had his own boarding school experience at Clongowes, not far from Dublin, and knew about a life without lockable doors. We locked what we could inside ourselves.

It seems unlikely that an undefended self could have survived these years, but I have high hopes of my 1980 diary. It is a brown, fake-leather book with '1980' in gold on the spine and embossed across the cover. I remember this physical object on the chair beside my dormitory bed, about the size of a Bible, and it has travelled in time between then and now. Here I am: *Richard J. Beard*, name and home address written inside the flyleaf. The diary has a lined page for each day of the year, and the style of my handwriting keeps changing: my character hasn't yet settled.

Here, in my private diary, I might have succeeded in preserving an honest, authentic self. That's what diaries are for.

It turns out that from January to March 1980, in the three months I managed to complete, my written self is a bit of a prig. I get the sense of a boy who feels under surveillance, frequently namechecking God, as if that's one of the criteria on which these pieces of writing will one day be assessed. Instead of insights into my thirteen-year-old self, the diary reads like another layer of hiding, a place where I can practise lying about my feelings. I use the elaborate vocabulary rote-learned in English lessons: *cacophonous*, *dilemma*. In the same spirit, I make sure to show off my rhetorical devices, especially alliteration: *lying lazily, frivolously finished*. Sometimes I do the vocab and the rhetoric at the same time: *discordant din*, and I never use one adjective when four or five will do. School is not school, it is *the vast abyss of knowledge*, as if I'm being paid by the word for the *Daily Telegraph*.

There are Latin tags, *tempus edax rerum*, as just one example of *verbal atrocities and general waffleness*, which I fear but seem unable to avoid. Aged thirteen, my diary reads as the prime minister speaks now, in his mid-fifties. I obviously feel obliged to fill the whole page, every day. Or what? What will happen if I don't? I have a totalitarian fear, as understood by Orwell, that by breaking rules I don't understand I can get into trouble. Even in private I therefore aim to replicate my idea of adult opinion. Television is *the root of all laziness*, and money *is the root of all evil*. I'm so wary of revealing myself that I reheat opinions either not mine or about which I know nothing. I'm a fan of Geoffrey Boycott and capital punishment. I'm against revolutionary movements and vandalism, modern verse and football.

Forty years later I get to raid the diary like the secret police, looking to prise out the innermost secrets of this elusive, clenched little boy. He claims the diary was *what I think and would not declare in public*. What a liar. What a lying toad he is. Anything true is accidental, like the insistence that *there is nothing quite like love. And my thoughts are that <u>real</u> love can only be in effect at home, where the family is*. This is from early January 1980, in the holidays after one night away at a friend's house. Back at school in February he receives a love note from a girl – *I love* ██, he writes, but the name is scored out to avoid ridicule from other boys. He has it all written down: *Paper is evidence, and evidence means conviction, and conviction means unpopularity.* He eats the note. He's not Winston Churchill of 10 Downing Street. He's Winston Smith of *1984.*

The diary labours to set out in writing what this frightened boy expects is expected of him, because children – like hostages – can get used to anything. *I love the house and the masters, the pupils and the Chapel,* says my 1980 diary. *The Chapel especially.* Liar. Putting name tapes in my clothes didn't help me stay who I was. In anticipation of the entrance exams I decide that Radley, which I know little about, is a *beautiful, friendly, kind, satisfying school.* What I'm saying is 'Please take me!', not yet confident that the public school pathway to power and glory is irrevocably mine.

A week later, on 23 January, I second-guess what I've already written. Aged thirteen and ten days I look back sadly on the diary of my poor twelve-year-old self, as I was in the first half of the month: *I now realise that the initial pages are rather childish.* Already, I was on the outside of the outside of myself. I wasn't really present, except, perhaps, in one bleak prayer: *Thankyou Lord for my 12th year that I have survived it.*

At least I was trying to find the words, because as Joy Schaverien puts it, 'without words ... the body finds a way of expressing distress'. I'd already had experience of this: in 1975, towards the end of the summer holidays, Mr Walters wrote me a letter.

6th September, 1975

Dear Richard,

I want you to be Pater this term to a new boy called Freddy Mecoy-Woods. You know I'm sure just what a Pater does, and I'm certain you'll make a success of your task. He will be arriving by car.

I'll see you on Tuesday afternoon.

Yours sincerely,

G. A. Walters

I was to be a *pater*, a father, at the age of eight. Actually, I didn't know 'what a Pater does', because since January 1975 I hadn't had the benefit of watching any real fathers in action, including my own. The pressure of faking the strong frozen emotions of a grown-up, not just for my own benefit but a boy even younger, proved too much too soon. By the second week of September I was in hospital with a mystery illness. It wasn't appendicitis, but they cut the appendix out anyway. Eventually, after about a month, the medical best guess was a twisted intestine – I wasn't able to digest what was happening to me. Then the intestine untwisted, or I decided boarding school was preferable to an open mixed-age ward in Swindon's Princess Margaret Hospital. As mysteriously as I'd fallen ill, I recovered.

Although this is an event I've never forgotten, I couldn't place it precisely in time until I found the illness referenced in my school reports. *Despite his illness ... a late start ... He now appears to have completely recovered from his illness and is once again his tough, cheerful and hard-working self.* It was 1975, near the beginning of my schooldays, and as the novelist Beryl Bainbridge once advised, get your breakdown in early and don't look back. I walked out of hospital and picked up where I left off, with my exterior toughness intact and plain on the surface for all to see. At school, I was going to be OK.

6

Teachers

'I have been in the scholastic profession long enough to know that nobody enters it unless he has some very good reason which he is anxious to conceal.'

Evelyn Waugh, *Decline and Fall*, 1928

The teachers at boarding school were *in loco parentis.* They took the place of parents twenty-four hours a day, for months at a time. Not simply teachers but schoolmasters, masters of the school. Most were men, and our parenting was contracted out to these half-fathers who stood in as role models. Look more closely, and maybe the parents hadn't thought this through.

'I expect you'll be becoming a schoolmaster, sir,' jokes the College porter in Evelyn Waugh's *Decline and Fall.*

'That's what most of the gentlemen does, sir, that gets sent down for indecent behaviour.'

At that time, as remains the case today, teachers in private schools were not legally required to have professional qualifications. As for experience, many of them remembered their years in these schools as boys. Sometimes the same school. They couldn't unfix themselves from the kind of institution that had formed them, and from the outside some of these men looked comical, or grotesque, or both.

After introducing the 1980 BBC2 Tuesday-night audience to a teacher in a gown, *Public School* goes behind the scenes into the Radley staff common room. It is a sanctuary of pewter tankards and severe side partings, hair combed in strict adherence to a directive issued in 1934. The younger teachers are less keen on the parting and fonder of hair over the ears, and this awkward straddle between the old world and the new helped make us the men we are today. Hair was a constant battleground. Too long, too short, too *individual*. Hair was a dialect among the school's many languages, a way of giving or withdrawing consent, and important enough for some of these children as adults to stay boyish in this way for the rest of their lives. Hair statements are a feature of twenty-first-century Tory politics.

As for the spoken language we shared with the teachers, I believed at the time that its strangeness would wilt and die outside the boarding school biosphere. Schoolmasters were fluent in their identification of *humbug, piffle, waffle, poppycock, drivel, codswallop* and *balderdash*. They explored variations on the theme of 'nonsense' to tell us we were lying or plain wrong. Like the Inuit people and their multiple words for snow, this vocabulary clustered around the subject of the teachers' closest attention. Boys were often in the wrong. Nothing we said was to be taken at face value and we were constantly in need of correction. '*Fiddlesticks!*' The teachers had many different ways of saying 'I'm not wrong, you're wrong'. *Tommyrot.*

We were *nincompoops*. We were guilty of *mumbo-jumbo* and *hocus-pocus, willy-nilly*. Among ourselves we were *swanks* or *squits*, or both, but the masters knew these words too. They said *tuck* meaning food, without wincing. We'd *duff* each other up or *do each other in*, but easy on the *aggro* or a teacher would have our *guts for garters*. Many teachers were vain about their language skills – *engage the cerebellum!* – yet could write end-of-term reports that were pure *gobbledygook*. This, apparently, sums up my performance in class for History A level:

> Were Rubens to produce his allegory of the aloof, intransigent schoolmaster lording it over this overtaxed history set, the young historian would certainly be holding the darts that Cupid threw – only here they are intellectually, historically, or even socially, baited.

The teachers didn't speak or behave like ordinary human beings, any more than we did. They had the same indifference to the texture and traction of contemporary reality, which was refused entry at the gates. In the closed world of the boarding school, the teachers too had their special names: Goat, Squaddie, Stavros. Like members of a cricket team (another collection of grown-up boys) they had a y or an o added to a section of their surname. Or in writing they were known by their initials, codes understood only by initiates: J.A.P. good, D.R.W.S. bad.

One memorable teacher at Pinewood, after Latin in the classroom, changed for afternoon games and trotted across the playing fields in long scout shorts and rubber-studded canvas hockey boots, his sinewy body rigid from the tops of his chevron-gartered long woollen socks to the shine of his brilliantined hair. He held his arms straight by his sides, his hands in neat fists with protruding thumbs, and when he stopped to talk to a boy he adopted a forward-leaning attention as if braced against a very strong wind. Was he about to hear some poppycock? He probably was. He turned his head to one side, so the balderdash could go straight in his ear.

What was striking, when I was first left at the mercy of strange men, was how many of them were killers. Commander Staveley taught French but had served during the war in the Royal Navy, as had Mr Robinson in the science lab. And as we knew from the *Commando* comics: *GRIMLY H.M.S CUTLASS TURNED TO FACE THE ENEMY.* In our minds our war veteran teachers had killed Krauts and Japs, though for Commander Staveley by the 1970s the sworn foe was any small boy who mispronounced the French word *squelette*. The sound of the squashed English u activated all his on-board sirens, but in exercising his authority he had the advantage of looking like General de Gaulle. That and his fondness for clipping children round the ear.

In my letters home I mention a maths teacher called Colonel Proudman, who despite his rank I don't remember, while the Royal Air Force was represented by Squadron Leader Hermiston ('Squaddie'), the handsome PE teacher in a white vest and slicked-back silver hair who'd flex his stomach muscles and say 'Punch me!' And for History and Geography we had Mr Lewis, who also supervised the rifle range, a dark damp space beneath some classrooms where we lay on dank mattresses to shoot .22 rifles in the prone position. We collected the brass cartridge cases and showed off our perforated targets, every bullseye our evidence we were ready to save the nation. Again.

Mr Lewis was the only teacher who talked about his war. He was a round, kindly man with broken capillaries in his cheeks – his skin seemed as traditionally British as his tweed jackets and checked shirts. His RAF career had contained two events of note. As a rear gunner, he had the most dangerous and therefore glamorous role in a Lancaster bomber, infinitely superior to the navigator who without a big gun served no obvious purpose. Mr Lewis claimed responsibility for the leather trim beneath the buckle of the standard RAF Bomber Command helmet. Once, coming down after a training flight at night, he was so cold that the metal buckle froze to the skin of his cheek. When he took off the helmet he stripped away the skin. He did have a red patch on the left side of his face. The other story he told was of the only time he fired his .303 Browning machine guns, at a German searchlight. He was so excited he used up every round of his ammunition, all in the one go.

On his other flights (and he was proud of completing his two full tours) he was never engaged by the enemy. This was not the derring-do of the trash mags, though clearly the Luftwaffe was canny in steering clear of future prep school geography teachers. Mr Lewis was my favourite, the substitute dad I'd have chosen as Dad. In the summer term, when the last lesson of the day was in mid-afternoon, he used to read aloud to us from Arthur Ransome as we waited for the bell and the release into cricket.

We had our war heroes too at Radley. In 2002 I interviewed Tony Money, at that time running the school archive but a long-serving teacher and former pupil from the 1930s. He died in 2008, but on that September day he was wearing a pale blue shirt, a claret tie and a grey, mud-coloured sports jacket. He had square tortoiseshell glasses and a high-domed head, a handsome small man in hush puppies and grey school trousers. Reluctantly, he told me about winning the Military Cross in North Africa for showing 'complete disregard for his own life', as reported in the official commendation. This was more like it. Mr Money had stormed a pillbox, tackled a German and then in the confusion was shot by his own men. At which point a grenade exploded.

'They threw a grenade at you?'

'No, I threw the grenade, earlier on. It rolled back down the hill.'

Over his long teaching career Tony Money taught five different subjects, an amiable killing machine sharing a common room with younger men and their disregard for traditional side partings. Mixed messages were therefore always a possibility, but to prevent nuance seeping out to the boys the staff presented a united front overseen by an all-powerful headmaster, more *Our Father* than *in loco parentis*.

In *Public School*, D. R. W. Silk, 'Dennis', is the star of the reality show. A former Cambridge rugby blue, he has broad shoulders and a big square head, and wears dark suits and tightly knotted club ties. He likes an ironed white pocket square, to match his shirts, and he once played county cricket for Somerset. As a youth he was therefore heroic, and it's perhaps unsurprising that in his study – a flower arrangement catches the flood of light through a stately window – he is more in sympathy with the past than the present. 'Too much too early kills,' he says. 'A bit of hardship is quite an important lesson to be learned.'

As he speaks, he screws his right fist into the palm of his left hand. Summoned to his study, I look at him with amazement: I am older now than he was then, this man who famously knew the name of every boy in the school, as if to suggest that he knew everything else about us as well. It was a power play. The respected Victorian headmaster of Uppingham, Edward Thring, capped his school intake at 330 – any more and he couldn't possibly know each of the boys individually. Silk, on the other hand, invited us to a meeting on our birthdays for an awkward few minutes of symbolism – *I know you* – smiling, repeating our under-used first names, fist inside the palm.

The Warden of Radley was such a forceful presence he was even scared of himself. He lived on Protestant time – never enough of it and stuff to be done, keeping himself busy as if terrified of standing still. Along with his headmastering, Silk was a JP and a school governor and on various MCC committees. He was a success in every way, which limited his opportunities to stop and think, and he adhered to the advice of the very first Warden, the Reverend Robert Singleton: 'the great thing was to be always employed, the devil hated industry'. A bracing daily momentum could buffet aside any overdue emotional reckoning.

Sometimes, we were paralysed by fear of these all-powerful men. Back in 1976, the junior dormitories at Pinewood were on a corridor along with the sickbay, and then on the other side of a fire door was the headmaster's private side of the house. One winter evening, in the dark after lights out, Goat Walters started bellowing. He sounded far away, as if he couldn't be bothered to leave his quarters. He was shouting the word 'Bullock', the name of a boy about my age who was in the sickbay, the room nearest the headmaster's staircase. 'Bullock!' he shouted. 'Bullock!'

Nobody moved, especially not Bullock, who had no idea what he'd done wrong.

The ageing headmaster was lying at the base of his stairs after a fall, his leg broken beneath him. Whoever eventually found him wasn't one of us. The boys were terrified of leaving their beds after lights out, stupefied in the grip of absolute power.

Boarding school headmaster was a leadership model closely observed, from the point of view of the child, by future CEOs and managing directors and newspaper editors and chairmen of the board and government ministers – the usual suspects. Pretend to know everyone's name.

Don't fall down the stairs. Unsurprisingly, the nature of leadership in a total institution repays the attention of Erving Goffman: 'Inmates very generally feel some sense of security from the feeling, however illusory, that although most staff persons are bad, the man at the top is really good – but perhaps merely hoodwinked by those under him.'

An all-powerful leader who escapes blame is a tantalising prototype, for a boy in training to lead. As Churchill himself lamented: 'Headmasters have power at their disposal with which Prime Ministers have never yet been invested.' George Orwell, creator of Big Brother, knew this at first hand from his prep school St Cyprian's, run as a dictatorship by Mr Wilkes and his wife, known respectively as 'Sambo' and 'Flip'. 'It was very difficult to look her in the face without feeling guilty,' Orwell writes, 'even at moments when one was not guilty of anything in particular.' Sambo and Flip's son, the Reverend J. C. Vaughan Wilkes, was Warden of Radley from 1937 to 1954. Sometimes known as Piggy, he caned more than 150 boys in a single day in the 'Great Gym Beating'. Coincidentally, the despotic leader in *Children of Men*, a dystopian novel by P. D. James, is called the Warden of England.

But it was the members of the headmaster's staffroom, the hoodwinkers, who were responsible for policing day-to-day expressions of conformity. And also for making sure that none of us were distracted from exams by thoughts of social justice. The idea was to transform laziness into endeavour, bad into good, boys into men. The slow would be made quick, and the quick more precise. Each individual self would be modified, hopefully for the better, and the most effective way to achieve this was to discourage boys from dwelling on their instincts and feelings. Just settle down and get on with it, as had generations of boys before us.

Tradition was one way the staff abdicated responsibility, and they had at their disposal, as a traditional means of exercising control, more awards and rewards than a banana republic. Prizes, colours, privileges, badges; I'm surprised we didn't have medals. At Pinewood I yearned for the blue-and-silver-striped tie for prefects. I wanted the hooped cap of the 1st XI cricket team, and the XI on a strip of cloth that could be sewn beneath my blazer badge for display on Sundays. At Radley there were ties for 2nd XI colours, *3rd* XI colours, house prefect, boat-club colours, and for the chosen few in the first teams, the tie *and* the scarf *and* the cable-knit jersey. School prefects had mortar boards with white silk tassels, a hierarchical symbol of who was up and who was down, preparing us for the politics of later life. Someone was always up or down, and it mattered.

Every boy from the age of eight was entered into a ranking process that never slept, like an educational strain of Puritanism. At Pinewood a *G* on a piece of homework earned one point, two for a *VG* and three for an *E*, an Excellent, so rare that the winner's name was read out at morning assembly. The minus points didn't need explaining in letters: −*1*, −*2*. Occasionally, full of doom, a −*3*. Not Good, Not Very Good, most disappointingly the opposite of Excellent. If the badges and colours and VG points were carrots, the minus points were a stick. And if that didn't work, the stick was a length of bamboo.

As a measure of our deference to power, Paul Watkins tells the story of Eton's top hats. During the Second World War, when the sirens sounded, the Eton boys were supposed to go running for the air-raid shelters. However, they were also traditionally punished for going outside bare-headed, so would stumble around in the blackout looking for their tall black toppers. They lived in such fear of authority that the teachers had to change a school rule to get them to run for their lives. After that, the Eton top hat never made a comeback.

In episode 7 of *Public School*, Dennis Silk happily confirms that a private boarding school 'doesn't set out to be a democratic institution'. He prefers the term 'paternalistic'. The trouble with this political model is that fathers come in a variety of types – on a spectrum from far too cold to far too hot. Some of the teachers did their best at the impossible task of standing in for parents. They made an effort to achieve the just-right level of warmth with home-brew evenings and bonhomie, but few real-life fathers invite their multiple unrelated sons into the sitting room (a special event, despite being sixteen years old) with the incentive of a bottle of home-brewed beer. Thank you, sir. At some point during this perfectly normal evening our ersatz dad would remind us of the name of his wife, who wasn't our mum. These occasions were like a best man's speech – everyone wanted it to go well, and therefore it often did. We returned the effort because we wanted the substitute dads to be true.

Less kindly stand-in fathers could be megalomaniacs, paranoiacs, fantasists, sadists. The round-the-clock hold of boarding school teachers allowed crackpot theories to develop unchallenged. As a young boy at Pinewood's long dining-room tables I learned, in earnest, from a desiccated teacher of classics, that people get fat because they drink water with meals. One should accept half a glass of water, out of politeness, but feel no obligation to drink it. Let that be a lesson for life.

Did any of them care? I'm sure they did, but the numbers were against them. Every surrogate son had too many brothers. In my last year at school, I self-medicated a boil on my buttock, avoiding the Infirmary because illness was a sign of weakness. After a fortnight it wasn't a boil but a seeping wound, leaking into home-made dressings of toilet paper and Sellotape, with aftershave as the antiseptic. I went weeks at a time without brushing my teeth, but no one was paying attention. I wasn't unattended out of unkindness, but unkinness: no one was family, all the time.

The staff too had their casualties. Out of favour, alcoholic, unqualified if intensely well read, discarded private school teachers can be found in the real-ale pubs of county towns quoting Shakespeare and Latin. They discover shamanism or conspiracy theories or a calling to write screenplays. Once plausible at the front of a class, they prop up the public bar and slur their lines. Andrew Motion remembers his maths teacher at Radley, Mr Catchpole, who shut himself in his room in the mansion house and swallowed a bottle of pills. 'Nobody found him until the holidays were nearly over, which meant his body had been up there for weeks, staring at the ceiling while the flies buzzed against the window.' And Christopher Hibbert tells the sad story of W. R. Smale, Tony Money's housemaster, whose teaching in the words of a colleague had become 'sadly digressive'. In 1941, after chapel, he gassed himself in his school accommodation. His suicide note read 'I am so lonely ... '

Hibbert calls the note 'pathetic'. I know what he means, but my initial reaction is to think he's using the word like a schoolmaster, to say 'girly', to say feeble and weak. What a wet note to write, when suicide was already such a weedy thing to do. Pathetic, in fact, what a pathetic little man.

To survive as a teacher, it wasn't obligatory to have a narrow world view, but it helped. In his 1980 end-of-year letter, the Warden blames a spate of shoplifting on the permissiveness festering in wider society and therefore beyond the control of schoolmasters. *We all know the difficulties in a society which worships affluence, where many of the young have far too many costly possessions and have experienced too much too early and find all the restrictions of school a great bore.*

On the outside a change in attitudes was under way, while on the inside the school's default political manoeuvre remained divide and rule, starting on the day of arrival by separating the boys into houses. At Pinewood we were issued with an elasticated snake belt, either blue or grey, and the prospectus cheerfully admitted that the two houses existed 'to compete with each other'. For Gryffindors and Slytherins, the Sorting Hat made selections by character, but at Pinewood we were 'Blue' in character or 'Grey' in character, and in my humble opinion the Blues had an aura of goodness about them while the Greys a touch of the night. Pit the houses one against the other in a permanent state of rivalry. And when the houses do come together, pit school against school.

While writing this, I've had the word martinet in mind. I've just looked up what it means: 'a person who demands complete obedience; a strict disciplinarian'. I think I've held on to the word because there's something toy-like and brittle about it – like a wind-up drummer boy that's easily broken. Roald Dahl thought 'they were tough, those masters, make no mistake about it, and if you wanted to survive, you had to become pretty tough yourself'. But actually they weren't that tough. They hid or sublimated their weaknesses, which then squeezed out in ways they couldn't always control. In 1979, interviewed in the school magazine, the director of *Public School* Richard Denton claims that some of the Radley staff deliberately obstructed his filming. He blames their insecurity, but then most of the teachers were housed by the school, on school grounds. The accommodation was a perk, but it was also a means of control – the teachers like the boys were trapped inside the organism. In term time they too had no other life than this, and adapted themselves accordingly.

At Pinewood in the late seventies an unmarried senior teacher lived on the same floor as the boys' senior dormitories. Opposite the top of the main staircase, his single room contained a single bed, a desk and chair, and beside the wardrobe two spare pairs of polished brogues. I'm inventing a bookcase and a comfortable chair, because I can't imagine a life without, but I don't remember them. The furthest toilet cubicle in the boys' bathroom was reserved for this teacher's use, and he sometimes walked across the landing in his pyjamas and tightly cinched dressing gown and leather slippers, washbag in hand, refusing to meet any boy's eye. He pretended this wasn't happening, and reality would resume when we were again fully dressed. We pretended right back. It was what we did best.

Pretence and performance were places of safety, for everyone. Our role models were teachers and teachers were actors, some more obviously than others, but they each had a schtick. At best the routine included kindness; a show of paternalism with the male schoolmaster as benevolent father. Occasionally the production was extravagant, and schoolmasters were always in danger of overplaying their version of themselves, becoming full-time cameos of 'sir'.

Not surprisingly, in *Public School* Richard Denton picks out one of these, the ham in the gown. Mid-fifties, round, florid of face, 'Goldie' flounces into a new boys' classroom and opens up his act. He is immensely pleased with himself, anticipating excellent reviews, but by then he'd put in the rehearsal time – since arriving at the school in 1950 there wasn't a day he hadn't performed this flagrant character to a captive audience. In *No Ordinary Place*, Christopher Hibbert provides an objective adult opinion: 'It was arguably true that Goldsmith came across as something of a buffoon.'

The television lens wasn't as deferential as awed thirteen-year-old boys, but within the walls of the school the eccentric was an indulged member of the teachers' tribe. Always good to have an additional escape route, and to survive a long career schoolmasters could scuttle into the hiding places of 'character'. Whims and eccentricities were a tolerated English affectation, in the right type of person secure at the top of the hierarchy.

Colourful, often unqualified teachers are part of private school mythology. Goldsmith was recruited by Wilkes who was the son of Orwell's Sambo and so on, back through fagging and beer rations to the tone set by men like Richard Busby of Westminster, who refused to doff his hat to Charles II. He didn't want his boys to think any man in the kingdom greater than their headmaster. In the absence of computer games and television, a bombastic teacher was a form of entertainment. However, a broad personality was also a protective shell, which in BBC documentary lighting was harshly revealed as 'personality'. Adults were not what they seemed, and H. G. Wells identified 'solemn puerility' as the curse of the schoolmaster – these teachers were serious but also childish. They could make our lives miserable but not always on purpose. Occasionally aware of the absurdity of their power, they sent themselves up with exaggerations and Latin: '*Carpe diem*, Johnson, *alea jacta est*!'

With their grown-up Latin they were forever stuck in a classroom at school, showing off – the trouble with the grown-ups at private school was that they weren't very grown-up. And some were such true believers they couldn't get enough of us, as in this letter from a teacher in 1978: 'I wondered whether Richard would be able to come down to Swanage in the summer holidays.' This was to a residential Christian summer camp, which I attended two years running, as if for the parents a full summer holiday with children was simply inconceivable. The camp was accommodated in a private school near the Dorset coast, school-on-sea except the teachers dressed down, meaning some of them took off their ties.

In 2017 it was revealed that the chairman of the Iwerne Trust, which organised these holiday camps for the privately educated, had used them to groom boys who at a later date he submitted to savage beatings in his garden shed. John Smyth made the boys confess to 'sins of masturbation', and told them they had to 'bleed for Jesus'. After the trust hushed up its internal report in 1982, Smyth left the UK for South Africa, where he became a religious campaigner against gay rights.

Christians as vicious as Smyth were not everywhere, but vigilance was advisable: every boarding school at this time was in danger of employing a paedophile, and in the canon of private school fiction sexual abuse is treated as collateral damage. It was at large in the habitat, something that could creep in at any time. Even Molesworth knows the danger is there: 'I should like to introduce a new master who hav joined us in place of mr blenkinsop who left sudenly.⁹' The footnote takes the reader to Molesworth's sly, cynical aside: '⁹, who would hav thort it he semed so nice.'

The journalist Alex Renton was at Ashdown House three years ahead of Johnson. In his book *Stiff Upper Lip* and the ITV documentary *Boarding Schools: The Secret Shame*, Renton tells the story of former Ashdown boys launching a civil case over historical sexual assaults by teachers at the school during this era. Renton himself had direct experience of the 'maths teacher who liked to rummage inside our shorts, offering us sweets in return for our silence'. When this teacher was moved on, he went with a reference to another private school. 'The crimes had been covered up, quite methodically, almost as though that job was covered in the *How To Run a Boarding School* manual.' As of 2018, there were thirty-one ongoing investigations of alleged sexual assaults at UK boarding schools, with 171 individuals accused of historical child abuse. Only half of the UK police forces responded to ITV's Freedom of Information request, so the total figure is likely to be higher. It is not a legal requirement for schools to report abuse allegations. Not then, not now.

They didn't love us, these men placed in the roles of our parents, but under pressure we could mistake what they did feel for love, because that's what as small boys we wanted so badly. As for my real father, despite the money he made as a builder, he once in his cups expressed regret for an unlived life as a bachelor schoolmaster in a boarding school. He'd only half wanted to live like his real dad, a builder, while the other half was drawn to his surrogate dads, an idealised image of a loved Mr Chips that glowed in the light of his Scotch and soda. He imagined himself solemn and puerile, respected by children more forgiving than his own.

I tried it once myself. Unqualified, with no previous experience, I was employed by an adult called Inky at a prep school with boarders in Oxford. The new boys, aged eight, were known as Little Men. I lasted a year and a term. No, I thought, no. I can't go through with this. Not again.

7

Values

'If public schools are national assets because of their leadership and training qualities, what are we to think of those qualities when we survey the mess into which their leadership has brought us?'

T. C. Worsley, *Barbarians and Philistines: Democracy and the Public Schools*, 1939

Like soldiers or horses, children needed to be broken – these schools broke us down, and then they built us up again. This was not a natural process. The man had to be made, which implied that boys were somehow unmade. We had something wrong with us, and punishable offences included being dirty, noisy, emotional or late. As in the military, the school would break the will of the wilful child until he no longer knew what he wanted. Until he didn't know who he was or what he felt.

Homesick? No, 'unsettled'. We'd get over it, until home became a fantasy, idealised and inaccessible. We should welcome the new reality, where we'd be told who we were and what we were allowed to want. Watching *Public School*, the swarm of positive adjectives comes thick and fast, reminders that the men the school is making will be 'courteous', 'honest', 'useful', 'happy', 'cheerful' and 'confident'. But 'not arrogant'.

Presumably, if private schooling was necessary, these were not the qualities we had on arrival. Boys fresh from home, in their natural state, were discourteous, dishonest, useless, unhappy, miserable and insecure. We were arrogant. In fact these negative adjectives are recognisable, not always inaccurately, as applicable to privately educated adults. Radley promised not to manufacture arrogant public school boys, not in 1980, because in the past that had been the obvious and observable outcome. Along with dishonest and miserable, and all the rest. Unfortunately, naming desirable qualities didn't automatically bring them into existence, however godlike the headmaster's powers.

A year after the film was made, in that end-of-term letter about shoplifting, the Warden explains that 'it was brought to my notice by the Police that a number of boys had been stealing from shops in Oxford and Abingdon and when I learned of the extent of the stealing I had no alternative but to expel the boys. In the main they had been stealing cassette tapes, but some "single" records and some fishing tackle were also stolen.'

What price those adjectives now? If in doubt, add some more. Evidently, boys also needed to be educated in justice and fair play, even though the schools we attended were unjust and unfair. It took an ingenious cast of mind to see how this would work. We'd learn the values of community, though the school in which we lived was lacking in women and girls and old people and poor people and babies. Other, more integrated communities had other, different values. Molesworth mocks the corporate blah that 'boys are encouraged to develop their individual characters and expand their personalities', exactly because the opposite was more likely: we'd run with the privileged herd as our inner self retreated inside a well-defended shell.

In episode 1, *Public School* sets out its stall with the Warden's speech to the new boys. The theme, picked up several times through the series, is his threat to instil 'habits for life'. These include habits of work, 'a habit that isn't terribly common these days', because we're lazy. Why wouldn't we be? Most of us will inherit money. The headmaster preaches the right habits for life because boys like us, who go through this kind of schooling, are famous as adults for a life of bad habits. We wreck Oxford restaurants, pay minimum wage, shift profits offshore and, keeping pace with the times, corrupt elections by misusing stolen personal data. We accept political appointments when we're clearly underqualified.

We aim to develop every aspect of a child's character.

Outwardly we learned Latin and the laws of cricket. The fortnightly term orders chart our progress in History and Scripture, Maths and English, but mostly we were absorbing attitudes. Every two weeks we were given an official percentage of rightness – *Science 61* – and a rank – $61^{4=}$. Better up than down, because the first will be first and the last will be last. We learned early to accept inequality.

In his essay 'The Lion and the Unicorn', Orwell advocates the 'abolition of all hereditary privilege, especially in education', and argues for a post-war settlement with 'safeguards against the re-appearance of the class system'. He wrote this in 1941, but by 1975 the pre-war, class-determined England had again floated to the surface. It couldn't be flushed away. The social injustice in education leaked through the nation, because what boys like us learned at school influenced the country we later put ourselves forward to lead.

In our isolation we learned that we were special. Everyone else was less special and often stupid, though with important distinctions: as privileged English-speaking white men we were sufficiently educated to appreciate that women and black people and the lower classes and foreigners could each be stupidly inferior in different ways. Some were guilty of *balderdash*, others of *codswallop*, and the segregation required to harden these attitudes called for a residential facility: this wasn't education so much as *re*-education, in the Maoist sense, easier to achieve if the process was at work twenty-four hours a day, seven days a week. Boarding school was where we went, aged eight, to learn to despise other people.

127

Better than women

The Warden aspired to paternalism. In my research, I haven't found anyone from a private boys' boarding school in this period offering a vision of maternalism. That was not what these schools set out to do, and there's a short hop, from the Latin to the Greek, to get from paternalism to patriarchy. We were brought up seeking the approval of men – few women were available to offer a second opinion. Women, in any case, were fragile and overemotional and frequently out of control. They were total girls.

I think mothers had the worst of it, like the victims of a traditional curse. Schools could advise mums to wear sunglasses at drop-off to hide their tears, and the boys responded in kind: showing any love at all was a risky business. From the first day onwards it was better to be a brave little soldier – *There are lots of new bugs and all there maters blub they hav every reason if they knew what they were going to.* I once saw a small boy screaming while horizontal with his hands clamped to the driver's door of a Volvo estate, while his father tried to pull him off by the legs. The mother sat in the passenger seat, and the next time she heard from her son it would be by post.

At Pinewood we had no access to a phone. In my house at Radley, before the 1989 Children Act, there was a payphone in a cupboard under the stairs, though by then our character-building was well advanced so we weren't in a hurry to use it. What difference would a phone call make? The mothers, in any case, were by now spectacularly othered. If they showed emotion they became the enemy. If they didn't, we were grateful and bereft. Loving mothers were a dangerous pollutant, whereas stoic fathers who hauled boys off car doors were heroes to be admired. These twisted standards weren't fair, but unfairness was what we knew.

I think of phoning my mum. I mean now, during the pandemic, because as an over-seventy she isn't supposed to be going anywhere. I decide against. I delay and defer. It's a sunny day so I go for a walk at the school. Later by email we agree to a Zoom call, because stuck in our shrunken worlds everyone has learned to Zoom. Then I don't send the link, because I realise I'd actually prefer to phone, compensating for the calls I didn't make as a boy. Too busy, too distracted, too fearful of emotional distress. On the baize pinboard above my desk is a black-and-white snapshot of Mum from the late seventies: Purdey haircut and long skirt, sitting in an upright deckchair on the boundary of the Pinewood school cricket pitch. Her arms are crossed in resignation as the cold creeps into her bones.

Mum picks up the phone, and I tell her I'm writing a book about boarding schools. We need to talk, I say, though it's a shame I can't come over, I can't come home to explain everything I'm thinking and feeling. She makes the obvious connection with the past and in the loaded silence, her breathing in my ear, I stare at her above my desk, in the distance beyond the boundary rope; she's pulling the two sides of her cardigan to overlap across her body.

'OK,' she says. 'Though if I'd known I'd have dressed up.'

129

The first question that enters my head is: 'What on earth were you thinking?'

So that's what I ask, but as an opening shot it sounds too sharp. I need to be more specific, ask questions that have factual answers. 'Whose idea was it?'

'It was your father's decision.'

'But what did you feel? Did you agree with the decision?'

'Do you remember how it was discussing things with your dad?'

From my schooling I recognise this as a rhetorical question. We both know the answer; with Dad we could discuss whatever we liked, but his original position wouldn't change. Mum tells me that Dad had friends who were sending their kids to private school. There were lots of tears on her side, but eventually they reached a compromise – yes to boarding school, but only the one closest to the house in Swindon. Using distance as the criterion for choosing the school meant that Mum was prepared to accept an all boys' school (at first with no day boys) where the headmaster had been on the staff since 1942. She didn't care. She wanted us nearby (seven miles via the A420), and within a year she was appointed to the school council.

'It gave me another excuse to come over.'

The physical presence of her boys was what she missed most, and this time, when she says this, I'm the one left hanging in the silence. Now as then we need to be in the same place at the same time to communicate properly, so when the lockdown restrictions ease I drive the Sunday end-of-term route from Radley village to Swindon. In this direction, homeward-bound, the journey always seemed easier and Mum's new bungalow is just round the corner from where we used to live. I feel like I'm going to the same place, until at the last minute I'm not.

These days Mum is alone in the house, just as she was as a young mother when her children were away at school. She hates being alone, and is pleased to see me. Together, over tea and half a home-made cake from the freezer, we try to reconstruct how she let that happen, engineering her aloneness at such an early age.

'We wanted what was best for you.'

I knew she was going to say that. And by implication Mum means better than the education she had herself. As a child, Mum was no stranger to total institutions. Her father worked in prisons, and she never stayed in the same school for more than eighteen months. She remembers her childhood through the map of his career, starting at Wakefield, a Category A men's prison, then Kingston in Portsmouth followed by Brixton. Mum lists other postings to Sudbury and Lowdham Grange, which were young offender institutions for boys between the ages of fourteen and eighteen, and I remember later Christmases we spent in the assistant governor's house at HMP Leeds.

'The first time I visited Radley I thought Lowdham borstal was cleaner and brighter.'

'How did you decide on Radley?'

'Dad decided.' Apparently he mistook the Warden Dennis Silk for someone else. Mum can't recall the details. 'By then I'd given up having an opinion because it didn't matter. I sound really wet. I don't think I was wet. I probably was wet. I wasn't as strong then as I became later.'

To fill the void when she felt 'pretty awful', Mum made herself busy. She banished her loneliness like a trooper, like the stoical schoolboys her husband wanted to make of her sons. She threw herself into her work on the school council, helped set up a hospice, a playgroup, did her bit for the West of England School for Children with Little or No Sight and was sworn in as a magistrate – her work rate was like Dennis Silk's, but as a former nurse who left school at fourteen. In her house without children she fostered disabled babies, her competence as a parent certificated by Swindon Social Services.

'I remember one of the first times we took you back to Radley, there was a Rolls-Royce outside the boarding house with a number plate that read ABLED.' I check that this is possible, because it seems so unnecessary, but someone could make it if they wanted to – A8 LED. They could if they had the money, and the attitude. 'I always felt out of place there, out of my depth. That was definitely when I lost touch with you all. You were growing up and I wasn't part of it.'

Her husband had been to a school like this and now her sons, and her sons' housemaster and teachers and headmaster were steeped in this all-boys experience. Suddenly there were a lot of men against one woman and Mum felt excluded. To our everyday values we added casual sexism – even as a school governor, a charity management officer, a foster-parent and a magistrate, Mum felt we looked down on her achievements as 'Mummy's little hobbies'.

'You mocked the way I spoke, and what I hadn't read. I was the little woman at home.'

I've never heard her say this before and I know it's true. After a few years at boarding school, undermining Mum became easier than loving her. What was a mother even for? She wasn't there when she was needed, and had utterly no idea about the properly restrained use of exclamation marks. Pathetic. Now, on the bookshelves of her house, on the mantelpiece, on the piano, she is surrounded by photographs of her grandchildren. She wants them in her life. I ask her if she's sad.

'We're not as close a family as we should be. That makes me sad. That's what it is.' She talks about her brother and sister-in-law, who for their adult children and grandchildren are a base and grounding point in times of turbulence and trouble. 'But you didn't have us from the age of eight, did you?'

We did not. Parents who sent their children away had to live with each other and with their regrets, but the mothers suffered most.

We needed our mothers, and to survive we rejected our mothers. When eventually we met women our own age, the dynamic wouldn't be so different, except at a boys' boarding school we didn't yet know this: we rarely met girls our age. This was not an accident. Post-colonial historians look at 'sublimating' as an animating force behind Empire-building, so that public school Englishmen, less distracted by sex than other Europeans, repurposed their frustration by conquering foreign lands. Or in writer and politician Wayland Young's phrase, 'love's loss is Empire's gain'.

The usual caveats apply: it wasn't as bad as it used to be. At Winchester College in the fourteenth century the all-male rule was rigorously applied – if a washerwoman had to bring back the laundry (as opposed to the preferred washerman), 'this washerwoman we wish to be of such age and condition as to be most unlikely to excite any sinister suspicion'. By 1980, these schools were not completely empty of women, like my piano teacher Miss Parkinson, as old as the century and right there next to me on the piano stool. But mostly the women were in marginal roles. At Pinewood we had two nurses with confusing motherly bosoms, and one term a young Australian intern with whom every boy fell in love. We had Iona and Pam in the dining hall, both disabled in some way, wheeling the trolley of jugs and mugs alongside the tables with their thick-lensed mantra of 'Tea or water? Tea or water?'.

For many schools at this time the economics of falling rolls meant that co-education became inevitable. Pinewood was down to seventy-eight boys and needed the fees. In 1977, a handful of girls arrived. The dormitory at the end of the junior corridor, nearest the headmaster's house, was given over to the girls, though few of the early intake were boarders. That made sense: day boys were girls in any case. Initially, nothing much changed and girls barely feature in my letters home. *I came 6th out of a class of fifteen boys and one girl.* In the final form order C. D. Kiamtia came first in English, History, Geography and Scripture. With the marks collated, she came first.

Apart from that, girls didn't disturb our friendship groups or interfere with important activities like games. They weren't going to be competing for 1st XV colours, if only because they left for secondary school when they were eleven, two years before we did. Girls felt inessential, like lessons in music or art. They didn't really count.

Except, having said that, I found myself open to courtly and hopeless love with my heart a heaving beating weight and in my diary *I love* ████. Before that 1980 diary entry, I remember a previous case of *I love* ████, the feeling so strong and pure I dared to arrange an assignation. Halfway down the corridor to the girls' dormitory was a shower room, and the first time in my life I was alone with a girl we both wore pyjamas. We stood side by side in the dark, out of sight from the doorway, leaning back against the wall with our shoulders almost touching. I didn't know what to say, or what happened next. I wanted to hold her hand. I wanted to stand there and hold her hand and then kiss her. Just kissing, in a nice way, on her beautiful cheek perhaps and then a little bit on her shoulder, on the nap of her flannel pyjama jacket. The thought of it made my chest and lips hurt. If I could kiss her then I'd always have kissed her and everything that followed would be different. We didn't kiss. The meeting was too strange, too intense. We were breaking school rules in a shower block at night in our slippers. But more than that, I was overeager for love. The moment passed. We shuffled back to our beds.

After puberty, in public school with no girls at all, the absence of reality left an open goal for sexualised fantasies. In another, earlier male-dominated environment, the penal colony of Australia, the humanitarian Caroline Chisholm agitated for the accelerated immigration of women and children, 'God's police'. They improved the moral tone, and would probably have deterred our Farah Fawcett posters and the tennis player not wearing pants. The young women we saw on a daily basis were two-dimensional objects on the wall, sold on from one boy to the next, though we didn't ache for them less.

We were courtly lovers and we were sex maniacs; there was no obvious middle ground. We studied Chaucer's *The Knight's Tale* while daydreaming erotic stories that started with an overarm serve. As fictions women were fantasy goddesses or unintelligible thickets of danger and disease. We were shown information films, which joined the dots to Randolph Churchill and his mystery illness in *Young Winston*. Sex led to pregnancy or VD, both of which threatened to interrupt a brilliant career. VD in those days was worse than STDs are today. It was every symptom at once, and the shame was incurable.

Boys of our era were very much at home, while at school, to the sexist hallucination of the *vagina dentata*. We had the Latin, and the fear of being taken in. We knew from experience that women were untrustworthy – look where our mothers had left us – so we kept watch, ill at ease, lecherously fascinated and appalled. Every woman was naked, but also imperfect in ways we had to look very closely to discover. If we weren't careful, women could be just another racket.

Girls needed to be defused. The 'girl' in the insult *don't be such a girl* was an imaginary composite of frailties we feared in ourselves, an emotional weakling who couldn't throw and couldn't run. She was as useless to us as the equally imaginary tennis girl was beautiful. Beauty wasn't so easy to neutralise. In *Public School* the Warden's adjective of choice for girls who visit the school is 'comely', and in the 1982 magazine the staff refer to their off-campus female private pupils as the 'lovelies'. There is the idea of a lure in both these words, with girls as sirens distracting boys from the one true path, which so far in our experience involved rugby and exams and strategic relationships with men and fellow boys.

And yet. We ached, ached for love.

At Radley there was one girl in the school, the daughter of a teacher, who was allowed to join in the sixth form. I picked my A levels to be in the same class, the same classroom. I fell astonishingly in love, as I had with my housemaster's daughter, because I was unimpressed by my boys-only life, as if girls existed at a remove from what mattered. I was fed up with aching at a distance, and in the minibus to the Goethe Institute, arms almost touching, I learned more about doomed German Romanticism than I ever would from the Kleist play we were travelling through the dark to see. I mean I felt the agony of love, felt it deeply, even though I hadn't the education to know what I was feeling.

What I did have was the education to get me a B in German at A Level, but the extra-curricular gaps had longer-lasting consequences. Professor Diana Leonard, who established the Centre for Research on Education and Gender at the University of London, published research in 2009 showing that boys from single-sex schools were more likely to be divorced or separated from their partner by their early forties. The mental health professionals, like Schaverien and Duffell, explain why. After those years of disconnection we can expect too much, every next woman an idealised promise of lost love regained. Our fantasies rarely survive contact with reality, and anyway, we have a tendency to wander. Making up for lost time, we want sex but come to resent women for our weakness for sex – as adults, erotic dependence becomes a new form of vulnerability to be resisted and denied like any other. Why couldn't women be more like an Athena poster?

We weren't cut out for relationships, in any case. Prematurely detached from our parents, we learned it was less painful to abandon before getting abandoned. Jump ship. Also, to be on the safe side, keep an emotional reserve. We needed to be sure we could survive alone if we had to, if we had to again. In these circumstances, emotional availability was a risk, and it was safer to stick with what we knew, a bleak deficiency of love. We made a habit of loving from afar, once the only option available. We couldn't grow up.

The title of Sonia Purnell's biography *Just Boris* (Kindle, £1.99) is a nod to *Just William*, Richmal Crompton's schoolboy who is aged an unchanged eleven from his first published adventures in 1922 until his last in 1970. Purnell sees that Johnson needs women 'to support, nurture and organise him'. Of his equally boyish contemporaries she says 'they all seem slightly in need of mothering, a bit vulnerable beneath the bluster'. 'Slightly' and 'a bit' are redundant here, but the curse on the mother extends to any woman later enlisted, temporarily or otherwise, to save us from the nasty men and the other boys. We wait in expectation of disappointment, as our childhood experience dictates, and usually we make sure we find it.

We try and we fail. We try again. The damage spreads out from the source.

Better than common people

We were made afraid to feel foolish, angry, loving, stupid, sad, dependent, excited and demanding. We were wary of feeling, full stop. Which meant that people not blessed with a private education were, compared to us, fizzing with emotions and therefore insufferably weak. How did the schools teach us this? The language was always chipping away – in *Public School* the boys casually refer to 'the lower orders', as if to a species difference, reptiles considering insects. Molesworth, of course, has a sharp eye for his teachers' attitude to 'oiks': 'Take no notice of them molesworth. They do not know any beter.'

Take no notice.

Along with Cameron and Johnson and others currently occupying positions of power, I was educated in the same extended private school era as George Orwell. We absorbed similar attitudes, and in 1936 Orwell decided to confront his Eton education by documenting the bleak living conditions of working-class households in Lancashire and Yorkshire. According to his biographer Bernard Crick, the resulting book – *The Road to Wigan Pier* – is an 'account of class prejudices instilled into a middle-class child'. Orwell's prejudices are not dissimilar to the ones instilled into me. 'Common people seemed almost subhuman,' Orwell writes. 'They had coarse faces, hideous accents, and gross manners, they hated everyone who was not like themselves, and if they got half the chance they would insult you in brutal ways.' Alien, dangerous, the working class evoked 'an attitude of sniggering superiority punctuated by bursts of vicious hatred'.

Anyone underestimating this divide should consider the evidence of the Radley College swimming pool, circa 1980. A story used to circulate that the pool was a yard shorter than a standard pool, so that no local swimming club would want to use it for practice or competitive events. Hibbert's history of Radley corrects this myth: the pool was deliberately designed a yard *longer*. The same reasoning applied. The locals shouldn't be encouraged. Typically, in a summer term ending in early July, we didn't swim in it much anyway.

In 1980, Radley's non-teaching staff were known as College Servants. We had cleaners, chefs, groundsmen, bit-part players and comic mechanicals. They represented the proles, the plebs, the oiks, the yokels, the townies and the crusties (a term Johnson continued to use forty years later). Our special language had its range of words to set these unfamiliar animals apart, meaning people not like us, and if you didn't know the language you were probably one of them. As George Orwell confirms in *1984*, 'The proles are not human beings.'

Round the corner from our house in Swindon was the Commonweal Comprehensive School. I can look it up on Google Maps – our front door was 0.3 miles from the local state secondary, a walk of two minutes. Our neighbours in the other side of the semi-detached house had children our age who walked there every morning. By implication, if my boarding schools were good, then Commonweal must be bad, and the thousand children who went there every day were not being properly educated. That stood to reason, or I'd be there myself. Even the name, presumably, was a lie. If it was for the common good, why wasn't it for me?

Because it was common. The clue was in the name. The unspoken suggestion was that Commonweal was everything a private school was not. We had to pay for development of character and good results, because these outcomes were unavailable round the corner. We also paid for physical and emotional security, even though I knew from experience that my private boarding school was physically dangerous and an emotional sinkhole. By comparison, Commonweal must be *lethal*. We rarely spoke to the neighbours. We acted as if we lived in a detached house, though we didn't.

I see now, thanks to outside location filming in *Public School*, that other boys were missing much grander homes than my own, but I'm not sure it made much difference. The missing was what was important. As for the effectiveness of my family's class laundering, if all went well I'd later look down on this place I came from, if ever I looked back at all.

From the colleges of Oxford and Cambridge, from the Houses of Parliament and the Inns of Court, from the Square Mile and from Lord's and Twickenham and from big houses in the country and from the high windows of the public schools themselves, we were trained to look down on everywhere else. The rest of the country was there but not there, and we passed through the in-between places with their in-between people on the way from one privileged stronghold to the next. We saw from car windows the petrol stations and primary schools and Bovis homes in which less privileged lives played themselves out, but the hopes and dreams of these people didn't meaningfully exist for us, nor their disappointments and pain.

This must be true, or when in power (which we usually were) we'd have brought these lives more in line with our own. In 1980 the Secretary of State for Education in Mrs Thatcher's first Cabinet (91 per cent male private school) was an Old Radleian, the Right Honourable Mark Carlisle. By way of the digitised school magazine, I can drop in on him that year in his office in the House of Commons. He is wearing a double-breasted pinstripe suit and a polka-dot tie, and his hair is swept back flat to his head in the style that Rik Mayall will soon be using as shorthand for Tory bastard. He has two grey telephones on his desk, side by side, and his narrow lips are squeezed tight and raised at one side. His is a family membership of the cult – 'Both my father and two uncles and two cousins and an elder brother went to Radley' – and he explains that the main focus of his job is to reduce public expenditure on state education.

Q. (from M.G.A. Scriven, 1980 editor of Radleian magazine): Don't the monied classes perpetuate their dominance in this way?
A. I don't accept the word 'dominance'.

When our isolation didn't make us vicious, it made us patronising. I remember a trip with an uncle to the Royal Tournament when I was about nine or ten, convinced that in London there were children who'd never seen a tree. I felt sorry for them. From the school itself our coach outings were to other private schools, theatres, museums or stately homes, safe houses for our kind of person. I used to enjoy these trips because in the packed lunches we had bags of crisps, like ordinary people.

Otherwise, our social segregation felt complete. The rationing of news protected the fantasy world of the school, where good was bad (love for a mother), and feelings (fear, sadness, bitter homesickness) were pushed aside to stew for later. In *For the Record*, David Cameron admits that about Brexit he 'did not fully anticipate the strength of feeling that would be unleashed both during the referendum and afterwards'. Of course he didn't. Strong feelings were involved, and also the common people. He was floundering in a pair of blind spots, to emotion and the British public. He gorged on a double helping of ignorance undisturbed since the days when his sense of right and wrong was shaped by which boys got to wear the fancy waistcoat.

Inside the boarding schools there was limited interest in where anyone came from – the fact of being there counted as credentials enough. I was occasionally derided as a *nouveau*, as in 'new money', but whatever social make-up anyone had when they arrived, we could expect to share certain fixed attitudes by the time we left. These included what the writer John Galsworthy called 'instincts of caste that forbid sympathy and understanding between the well-to-do and the poorer classes'. In *The Old Boys*, an excellent history but unconvincing apologia for the public schools, David Turner describes the status of private education at the turn of the twentieth century: 'It was not a caste system, since a wide variety of boys could attend if their fathers could pay. It was, instead, an island connected to the vast mainland of British society only by narrow and badly paved bridges.'

That island was no better connected eighty years later. Our sense of community wasn't with the rest of the country but with boarding school boys back through time, mostly white and rich, with whom we shared an essentially stable experience. Given our easy route to power and privilege this *was* a caste system, with hierarchical assumptions not dissimilar to those George Orwell categorised for Germany in the 1930s. In Germany, according to Orwell, the hierarchy went Nazi Party, German populace, conquered white people and finally 'the coloured peoples', as slaves. The caste hierarchy assumed at an English private school in the late seventies and early eighties differed only slightly:

English private school boys
The great British public (including, when expedient, British women)
White, English-speaking foreigners (from the former colonies)
White foreigners (Europeans)
Brown and Black people

Orwell sees this assent to human inequality as the core of fascist ideology. Segregated from the community, white public school boys grew up separately from 96 per cent of the population. At boarding schools we embraced the idea of English exceptionalism, and even among the extraordinary English we were the chosen few, elevated above the masses to perform great tasks. Leadership was a form of 'service' assumed into our approved conservative world view – traditionally we were the leaders, and we saw nothing wrong with that.

Shortly before the 1983 general election, the one following my prediction of the historical impossibility of a Tory victory, the Warden gathered the boys together for a special assembly. He wanted to warn us about the left-wing leader of the Labour Party, Michael Foot. His tone of voice was the one he reserved for the most disappointing boys of all, not smokers or drinkers but socialists. Michael Foot threatened our privileged way of life, a notion both wrong-headed and evil. Few of us were of voting age, so the Warden wasn't asking us to vote for Mrs Thatcher but to share a consensual view among right-minded adults. We needed to be told how to place ourselves in relation to the politics of the day. This was consistent with the complacency of a century earlier, when according to Hibbert, the Radley College Debating Society was 'never very lively since few boys could ever be found to present other than Conservative views'. At that time the motion 'Should the lower classes be educated?' was soundly and predictably defeated.

By 1983 I didn't care, not like I had in 1979. I'd given up and was going with the flow. We were superior, so it followed like night after day that everyone else was inferior, especially the working class and whoever ventured to represent them. Nick Duffell, in his book *Wounded Leaders*, argues convincingly for affirmative answers to the following rhetorical questions: 'Could it be that the British working class as an entire group have been suffering projective identification from the upper classes? Have they been standing in for the stupid, messy, incompetent children the latter wish to distance themselves from in their own collective psyche?'

'It *is* divisive,' says Warden Silk about private education in *Public School*. He's a JP, he's a future president of the MCC; he's not stupid. Social division was the whole point. If these schools didn't divide *nouveaux* like me from the place I'd come from, they wouldn't be worth the money.

During our suggestible younger years we were educated to think of ourselves as superior and not inferior people. In 1987 Richard Denton directed a half-hour follow-up documentary, *Public School Update* (also available on YouTube) in which a boy from the original Radley film, now a student at Oxford, laments the fact that he's an 'all round man – mediocre at everything'. The school should have taught him to be brilliant, and despite the self-deprecation his educational background has conditioned him to reject mediocrity. Only a few years out of school, he isn't yet aware of the psychological stress of repressing whatever it is that makes him feel inferior.

Instead, like the boys that had gone before, he too feels entitled to lead and to influence brilliantly and to claim his place in the Public School History of England. As a caste we were responsible for every English triumph, though also, if truth be told, for every calamity, because we were invariably the people in charge. Our tradition of leadership continued not because we had a talent for it, but because we resisted giving anyone else a go. We kept putting ourselves forward, believing that we were the best people for the job. The ruling master race, such as it was in Britain, was ours to join.

By 1979 I thought the days of such arrogance and iniquity were over. I was wrong.

Better than black and brown people

If master race Nazi English public school boys seems an exaggeration, then maybe it was, ten years earlier or later. I can only speak with authority for the period that educated the boys who ended up in charge of the country from 2010 and into the 2020s. *Public School* shows a mock hustings that shadowed the general election of 1979. By then, boys had been found 'to present other than Conservative views', like the candidate who stands for the National Front. He makes his speech on a flat roof above a crowd of cheering teenagers, all of them male and white. At the next general election in 1983, I learn from the school magazine that the hustings include not one but two extreme right-wing candidates, representing the 'Radley Right-wing Party' and the British Union of Fascists, which campaigns on a platform of 'deporting all blacks'. After the rabble-rousing speeches the school allows a separate indoor event for candidates to summarise their views. *The evening was dominated by Rolfe Hayden who marched in late wearing black SS uniform.*

It was a laugh, presumably. After the broadcast of *Public School*, applications to Radley soared. At much the same time, in another prestigious private school seventy miles to the east in Dulwich, a teacher was writing to her headmaster to advise against making Nigel Farage a prefect. The boy had 'professed racist and neo-fascist views', and according to another member of staff Farage had marched through a Sussex village singing Hitler Youth songs. The headmaster dismissed Farage's behaviour as 'naughtiness'. Another Dulwich teacher conceded that Farage was 'a fascist, but that was no reason why he would not make a good prefect'.

In the Pinewood sports team photos from Mum's attic I can count the darker faces on three fingers of one hand. We had two brothers recently arrived from Nigeria, and the son of an Indian doctor who lived not far from my parents in Swindon. At Radley one boy in our year was possibly mixed race – we didn't really know but mocked him for it anyway – and among the gods was Andrew Harriman, star of the 1st XV, who later played rugby for England and captained the World Cup Sevens champions of 1993. The other dark faces we saw were in *Zulu* and *Young Winston*, where savage natives were subdued by the civilising force of white British warriors. Did that turn us into racists? Yes, I think it did.

In the holidays I'd go to the post office on Victoria Road to collect Mum's child benefit, and when the British Asian post office worker stamped the book I was immensely pleased with myself for acting as if he were just like anyone else. Also, the 'possibly mixed race' boy in our year was Chris Sheasby, another future England rugby international. In my sports reports in the school magazine I make feeble gags about Brownian motion and Sheasby 'blacking' other players. I don't even know what that means, beyond the racial slur. The supervising editor of the magazine, a teacher, saw nothing in need of editorial attention. And why would he? The racism was institutional, and in 1982 after the visit of an American choir, the Warden writes to the parents that 'I will remember particularly the jazz pieces sung by four prehensile negroes'.

The only physical fight I had in either school was with the older of the Nigerian boys. Why him? I must have believed a black Nigerian couldn't be placated like an Englishman; he was to be treated as differently as women or the working classes. I don't know where he is now, but I find the son of the Indian doctor on LinkedIn – Ravi is successful in business, though he asks me not to use his real name. Whatever I think about private schools and racism, what does he think?

Initially he's cautious. He writes back that 'frankly there are some very bad memories of that time that are very painful ... not sure what you want to address here'. I explain what I'm writing, and how our schooldays involved attitudes to class and gender and race that have wider implications, but I appreciate that after forty years I've popped out of the internet and flung this baggage head-high at a virtual stranger. Eventually, we speak on the phone and I see Rav as he is in a recent interview on a YouTube business channel. Black suit, grey shirt, plain blue school tie, a handsome man of my age with casually unbuttoned cuffs and fast hands to put his thoughts in order as he presents them.

As first-generation immigrants, he tells me, his Indian parents wanted to give him a good education, though he admits his experience was 'mixed'. He genuinely didn't sense racism at Pinewood, though he remembers the school, in a good-natured way, as 'brutal'.

'God, the first week. Sneaking. Getting sent to Coventry. Talking to the nurse and standing outside for three hours. Then getting beaten. Looking back it's insane.'

Like me he had sport to redress the balance, and admiration for one particular teacher, 'the best teacher I ever had'. Overall, Pinewood was 'pretty decent'; his public school less so. He asks me not to name it.

'I was called a wog and a Paki. There was the National Front.'

'Sorry?' I ask him to go back to this.

In his school as at mine public speaking was encouraged – good for the confidence – and one boy was 'passionate about the National Front'. Rav regrets sitting in the audience and at the end of a hate speech clapping politely, demonstrating the good manners he'd been educated to value. 'You had to fight. The bullies were weak people, all the weakest and unpopular people.' There was also racism from the teachers, in remarks that casually encompassed Rav's father and family.

Having said that, Rav doesn't feel like a victim, not like his friend at another boarding school who was 'smashed to pieces, massively abused', presumably by boys who today are likely to be in positions of authority. From his own public school, Rav has three or four lifelong pals, and wants to acknowledge his privilege, despite the discrimination. In east London, for example, Indian boys had it worse.

'The whole point of private school education was to have confidence. That's what you're buying.' This and other brochure benefits – 'loyalty, friendship, morality' – and Rav feels he got a fair dose of them all.

We talk about our university-age kids, and the challenges they face. For our generation university was free, employment was accessible and property-owning not unthinkable. Nothing there that political leaders with an education like ours considered worth conserving. But Rav keeps veering back to our schooldays.

'We have got some issues, without a doubt. Not sure what they are, various things we're not very good at ... emotionally stunted. Maybe we are.'

Rav didn't board until his last terms at Pinewood, and his public school experience was improved by co-education. He does know some boys who boarded from an early age: 'There's no question there's psychological damage,' he eventually says. 'It's self-evident. No doubt about that.' He chose to send his own children to private schools.

Just better in every way. Exceptional, in fact.

Our vocabulary betrayed our sense of superiority, because our stock of disparaging words included everyone who deserved our scorn, like poofs and homos. This was particularly hard on a boy called Gay, who was also a day boy. As long as we weren't girls, swots, oiks, wogs or queers, we could be jolly decent chaps.

All those other categories were synonymous with weakness, to be joshed without mercy by the strong. And if a boy struggled with the spontaneity of banter, he could memorise jokes about the Irish, who were unbelievably thick. We laughed at anyone not like us, and the repertoire on repeat included gags about slaves and nuns and women hurdlers. One September, after a boy came back from a holiday in Australia, we had jokes about Aborigines. We internalised this poison like a vaccine, later making us insensitive as witnesses to all but the most vicious instances of discrimination.

And while we were down there, not to exclude any vulnerable minority, we frequently called each other spaz. You spastic. You loony. *Durr*, with a slap of the hand to the cheek, or the side of the head. Schizo. Everyone who was not us, a boy at a private boarding school from the late seventies to the early eighties, was beneath us, including younger boarding school boys who had life so much softer than we did. Obviously we too were a minority, but of all the minorities we were the most important. Of course we were. We'd end up running the country.

8

Escapes

'Once a boy have been sent to a skool the die is cast.'
Geoffrey Willans, *Down with Skool*, 1953

Here I am, up at Radley on a sunny day on the public footpath outside the old History classrooms, evidence of how hard it is to escape. We're all still here, though some of us more literally than others.

A quick update on the national situation: not good. Great Britain is on the brink of disaster, again. Our private school leaders are looking for a way out for us, but as things stand they haven't done a great job of reassuring the fearful or empathising with the relatives of the dead – a detached observer will have noticed their blunted ability to feel for the discomfort of others. The country continues to wait, mostly patiently, for political decisions made according to the economy or the science. Sure, but also according to what kind of politicians have taken back control, meaning the kind of people they were educated to be.

While the prime minister bluffs and stutters, at least the weather has been kind – the driest April and May on record – and in the spring sunshine Radley's immaculate buildings have something they want to say: despite the erosion of a once great country, these schools are remnants of the English past that flourish undisturbed. The tide of Empire has receded, leaving the public schools upstanding and intact, rich with the loot of hundreds of years and unassailable in their record of shaping the fate of the nation. I should be entranced; I should be so lucky.

Every time I walk here the facilities – the new observatory, the rowing tank, the Silk Hall Theatre – remind me of the characteristic that distinguishes these schools most clearly: they have more money. This isn't a secret. In 1980 the Friends of Radley Trust, along with the Warden, sent out a letter to new parents affirming their unity 'in wanting Radley to become a better and better school'. There is 'one tangible way in which you can help us', they write, which uninspiringly turns out to be by sending more cash. In addition to the fees. 'Please do so if you possibly can.'

At exactly the same time the Secretary of State for Education, Old Radleian Mark Carlisle, didn't think that reducing expenditure would make state schools worse and worse. In a failure of simple reasoning the money logic only applied to us, and from these old school begging letters I've learned how every added facility was justified. In 1983, the Warden feels 'very strongly that anything that helps break down the mystery and elitism of the independent sector can only do good'. On that occasion, he wanted to break down elitism with top-up contributions for the golf course.

No wonder school and not-school began to diverge as competing realities. In early June 1977, summer half-term, we celebrated the Queen's Silver Jubilee with a street party in Swindon, though of course we were strangers to the children in our street. The Commonweal kids were so unironic that they didn't understand the premise of my dad's slow bicycle race, or why the rich private schoolkids had Moulton Minis coveted by absolutely no one. Basically we didn't need cool bicycles; we were never at home to use them. On their Raleigh Grifters the neighbours rushed off the start line, heads low over the handlebars, legs pumping. It was a race, and they wanted to win. But we set the rules, and by coincidence we had the right equipment. On my Moulton I was the winner by a street, coming in very slowly indeed to no applause whatsoever. What a terrible day that was.

Gradually, the controllable, sheltered artifice of school became the more significant reality, and at some point we forgot what was so great about home. It used to be the freedom to rush in from primary school and dress as a cowboy before a teatime of scrambled-egg sandwiches and a wrapped chocolate biscuit. I remember a summer soon after starting at Pinewood when I was in the garden at home embellishing some randomly improvised adventure. I promised myself I'd really get into this, and commit myself fully, the next time I was home and it wasn't the school holidays. Then I realised, shockingly, that from now on there was no time at home not in the holidays.

A force field intervened, meaning that home was an idea just out of reach. Home and school had few points of contact, and in a further perversion of reality it didn't help that getting sent home was framed as a punishment. Going home was the worst thing that could possibly happen, as stated in the Radley College Statutes dated 1 May 1939, but decidedly still in force:

STATUTE 46. If the Warden, whose judgement shall be final, is satisfied upon due inquiry that any boy has committed a grave offence, or has been wilfully and persistently idle or disobedient, he may expel such boy forthwith or request his parent or guardian to remove him forthwith or at the end of the current term, and such boy shall be removed accordingly.

Go home. Live with your parents. Feel the horror, the disgrace.

We could go home voluntarily, of course, on our limited schedule of permitted Sundays, but our assimilation into boarding school life could be measured by the awkwardness of these exeats. *Dear Mummy and Daddy, Thankyou for taking me out on Sunday. I am looking forward to coming out again.* We thanked our parents, in writing, for seeing us once a month, though we could also be rescued by parents who weren't our own. 'In addition to these outings, I do allow boys to go out with their friends.'

Dear Mummy and Daddy, I deepfully regret that I will not be able to come out next Sunday unless it is because of guests etc. This is mainly because I would very much like to go out with McDonald.

We accepted as many of these invitations as possible. They were a sign of popularity, which like everything else was a competition, but the parents of other boys were less toxic, in terms of provoking homesickness, than our own. It wasn't like going home; it was usually better than that. These other families had fun dogs, motorised go-karts, crisp roast potatoes. On farms there were mushrooms to pick for lunch, a barn with stacked hay bales to climb, maybe even a wall against which to kick a football. Back at school, we lost contact with the feeling of 'home' as we did with so many other feelings.

Could anyone escape this fate? Some boys had more of a chance than others, often outsiders saved from full immersion by social class or skin colour. They were more likely to be able to keep their distance from the worst of the damage. Other individuals could be rescued, abruptly, by a trauma outside the control of the school – a more urgent reality intruded, and by comparison the pretensions of boarding school were revealed as flimsy and unconvincing. None of us were *supposed* to escape, considering how much it cost and how much good it was supposed to do us.

I have vague memories of a boy or two attempting literal breakouts from Pinewood. Train stations were involved, and capture and return, so I may have confused World War

II with life. More pragmatically, the fantasy of escape was restricted to a midnight walk. Towards the end of the summer term, strictly at midnight, we used to climb out of the senior dormitory window onto a fire escape. We were setting ourselves free, in a small way, and once at ground level with our bare feet in the grass we could have gone anywhere. Conifers shivered in the moonlight. We sought out shadows and crept towards the tennis courts, hearts hammering. Nothing much was happening at five past midnight near the tennis courts. We stalked across to the playing fields. Sick with excitement and anxiety, the realisation dawned that we didn't have anywhere else to go. The school was all we knew, and we might as well head back to bed.

Escaping wasn't so easy. One of the POWs who tunnelled out of Stalag Luft III, as fictionalised in *The Wooden Horse* (a regular Saturday-night film), was an Old Radleian. He'd been planning something like it for years. Oliver Philpot's subsequent book – *Stolen Journey* (1950, hardcover, £235) – has illustrations by Ronald Searle, who would soon get the gig drawing Molesworth for Geoffrey Willans. This was another reason escape was difficult. We were in, and our parents were in and our friends were in and the politicians were in and the illustrators of our favourite books were in; there didn't seem an obvious way out.

And even if there were, the escape committee couldn't be trusted to provide a convincing civilian disguise: I doubt I wore trousers of the right length more than once or twice a year, like a stopped clock. In Swindon our ill-fitting clothes made us into increasingly visible misfits. My home clothes were too small, because I grew when I was away, and my school clothes were too big because I was expected to grow into them. And then the other way round. A change into 'weekend leisure dress' for a Sunday out, as stipulated in the Radley school rules – *a) An open neck or casual sport shirt or monochrome T-shirt, b) Blue jeans or slacks, clean and inoffensive* – felt as proscriptive as a second uniform, school extending its reach. Brogues and jeans, a belt and smart shirt, some of these boys had their dress code for life.

Even now I can feel trapped. I'd prefer my past to be less troubling to me, and I know that to look back too intensely is to offend the instinct of the tribe. Don't make a fuss about nothing. Don't feel it. Don't say it, because the other boys might laugh. By trying to escape, I expect to be mocked – *Where's sad Rich Beard to open the batting? Oh, he's on a journey into his past.* In his novel *England Made Me*, Graham Greene has the unreliable, amoral Anthony Farrant ruined as a human being from the turning point in his childhood when he returns to boarding school instead of persevering with a literal running away. In later life his sister regrets sending him back 'to conform, to pick up the conventions, the manners of all the rest'.

Outside of fiction, the running away could take various surrogate forms. I'd tried a mystery illness in the autumn of 1975. Five years later, during the first term at public school, I had a relapse. I went to the Infirmary, a building beyond the chapel which offered less emotional warmth than I'd hoped for. I lay on a bed for a few hours and the mystery pain disappeared. The rebellion of the body hadn't worked earlier, so why would it now? My head overruled my gut, and put my innards back in their place. The desire to be well, or at least 'to conform, to pick up the conventions', was more powerful than dissent and the urge to go home. I'd have to learn to escape while staying where I was.

Though only a partial escape, organised games were definitely a useful distraction. T. C. Worsley, in *Flannelled Fool*, soothes his wounded sensibility with cricket: 'behind the pretence of virility which cricket and other games supplied ... it enabled me to escape noticing what in fact I was missing'. At boarding school all but the most stubborn hold-outs get the bug, in some form, for games. In his autobiography *Boy*, half-Norwegian half-Welsh refusenik Roald Dahl includes a photo of himself aged eight in his prep school days. He's at the cricket nets in his dressing gown and pyjamas, taking a middle-stump guard. In his caption he identifies himself as Jack Hobbs. Dahl is escaping from school, away not with the fairies but with the English cricket team at Lord's, in 1924.

Sport transported us, and not only for a moment. If we couldn't play, we escaped into imaginary cricket matches scored in *The COMPACTUM Cricket Scoring Book (100 YEARS OF SCORE BOOKS 1877 – 1977)*. On 6 May 1978 I pitch the World XI against the World XI 2nds. Witness the effects of my competitive schooling – I gather together the best twenty-two cricketers in the world and put some of them in the 2nds (including Dennis Lillee and Barry Richards). Given the choice between reality and games, games were preferable even when hijacked for the purposes of the total institution. Christopher Hibbert quotes the Warden's preference for 'hard and serious games' that would introduce boys to 'disappointment and failure without much risk of damage being done'.

In fact, at best, games were a daydream of escape. As were the sketches of warplanes that over the years morphed into guitars, the curves of the Telecaster as approximate to reality as those earlier Heinkels. Every doodle in the margins of a ring binder was a fleeting getaway, the equivalent of reaching for the outside world by digging a tunnel with a teaspoon, one daydream at a time. We were all in favour of escapism. The most proficient could reach 'a special kind of absenteeism', identified by Goffman as a feature of total institutions, 'a defaulting not from prescribed activity but from prescribed being'. Much of the time we were there, but we weren't really there.

We started out on our infuriating histories of absence, of distraction. Despite the Warden's best intentions, here was an enduring habit for life. We escaped from constant scrutiny and supervision and competition into our one film a week (*The Land That Time Forgot*), and then later into Sunday-night television, *The Professionals* or *Brideshead Revisited*. Act in a play. Volunteer as an altar boy. Become obsessed with biker boots and crimped hair. We tapped at the walls searching for a weakness, a way out to offset the school's intrusion into those secret places necessary to protect the self. We read a lot of books.

In both schools we had a library and a bookshop, though the range of titles was limited. A letter home in 1978 tells me my current library book is *The Cricket Match*, my horizons at that stage not obviously broadening. We devoured

162

our trash mags – BRAND'S MISSION WAS OVER. FOR HIM, LIFE ITSELF WAS OVER. BOB RUSHED OVER TO SEE IF THE TOP BRASS WERE SAFE – and subscribed to *Warlord* magazine (first published in 1974) for the comic-strip adventures of Lord Peter Flint. We binged on the Hornblower novels set during the Napoleonic Wars. I was also fond of the racist, anti-Semitic gentleman-adventurer Bulldog Drummond. These thrillers were written by H. C. McNeile under his pseudonym 'Sapper', between 1920 and 1937.

I could buy a more recent novel from the bookshop, which I remember as a triangular cupboard in the library that looked like an outsized metronome. I bought *Lord of the Flies* (1954) by William Golding, but for lighter relief the lower bookcases in the Assembly Room were filled with *Punch* magazines. The issues were bound in tall regiments of burgundy covers with gold lettering, dating from the 1890s through to about 1965. On high days and half-holidays we were allowed to take these out and skip through the cartoons, and I was familiar with line drawings of Anthony Eden and handsome Harold Macmillan, with his downturned eyes and moustache. Through these cartoons I knew more about Suez and Dr Beeching than I did about the Winter of Discontent. Politics was such a joke! It was something to laugh at, twenty years too late, or maybe twenty years too early.

Even the escape of reading could be made competitive. Bernard Crick, Orwell's biographer, reports that at his hated prep school Orwell won a prize for 'best list of books taken out of the library'. In my letters home my reading seems guided by a similar spirit – *On the reading chart I am on Number 3*, but inarguably I was also making my getaway with *The Otterbury Incident* and *The Heights of Zervos* and *Tales of the Greek Heroes*.

Still too deeply in? We tried expressing our sexuality, an escape that can last a lifetime, whichever way it goes. For boys in a boarding school this meant masturbation and homosexual curiosity, a form of escapism not as common as sometimes believed, or as the Warden in *Public School* says, 'grossly overplayed'. No one wanted to be a homo, so homoeroticism was squeezed into the clumsy transitions between banter and roughhousing. I did once see, from a doorway, a naked dormitory captain, aged about thirteen, standing against a wall being masturbated by younger boys. In my memory he is restrained against his will, but on reflection I think he probably wasn't. That was just my interpretation of his arched back and his thrown-up hands and the grimace on his face. To witness this performance was like watching a chemistry experiment. Here was an older boy who could 'produce', whatever that meant, and it was as interesting to observe as the heating of ammonium dichromate. Otherwise, during my nine years of living in boys' boarding schools, I had a penis in my mouth no more than once. If you were curious you could find out more. If you weren't, you wouldn't.

Later on we drank, we took drugs. Poor Cameron was caught on an island in the Thames, the Queen's Eyot, smoking spliffs. He had to go home to the Old Rectory for a while, to think seriously about what he wanted to make of himself: alas, despite this early attempt, he could never get out of his private school head. The next term he was back at Eton on the straight and narrow. After a little thought he repressed those rebellious urges as he had so much of his inner self since the age of seven, and from then on he repented and did what was expected of him. He became prime minister.

With drugs, as Cameron discovered, if the school caught us first we were beyond the reach of the law. In these instances the police were rarely involved, and therefore in the bigger picture we learned that for people like us the law was negotiable. The school took crime and punishment into its own hands and our escape attempts were belittled as scrapes and japes, escapades to be treasured later as old-boy anecdotes. I saw boys stupefied in their cubicles after inhaling aerosols through towels. That was a thing for a while, but I don't know where they went in their stupor, or whether it was a better place to be.

To get drunk, we went to the Junior Common Room, a bar for teenagers in the cellars below the historical Georgian mansion. It couldn't have been sunk any lower, possibly not far from Sewell's ghostly Whipping Room. In theory we were allowed one pint of beer twice during the week and two pints on a Saturday, but with an unusual lack of curiosity Christopher Hibbert claims that after its establishment in 1970, 'this privilege was not known to have been abused for some twenty years'. We behaved terribly, but learned that our bad behaviour was consequence-free, even though not all of us had given up hope. Unlike Goffman's asylums and prisons, at a boarding school behaving badly was a way to get out, to get sent home.

That's what I think was happening with my friend Ben Hinchliff. The son of a Yorkshire farmer, I don't know how he ended up at a boarding school in Oxfordshire, but few of us talked about our families. We preferred the self-deceiving notion that we'd landed fully-formed from the sky – if we couldn't be free we could at least be unattached. Well into his teens Ben scuttled round the school in a straight-legged lope that cut short the wastefully slow breaks between the more interesting places he needed to be. He had that kind of extreme absenteeism I envied, with books to read and his guitar to play and his homesickness to banish in the moves of early Mick Jagger. To my mind he was much more convincingly not public school than I was – the farm near Sheffield trumped the Swindon semi-detached, or so I thought. I liked to cast Ben as my better self, convinced that no matter what I did or where I went, he'd get there first. He'd make a better fist of life, because he was smarter than I was and played less safe.

Like Johnson at Eton, Ben was selected to edit the school magazine. He wrote brilliant short stories about cows, and the cigarettes he stole from his grandma. He was also a boy who got drunk in the cellar JCR, hurling his darts at the dartboard, burying the tips as deep as his disgust at the person the school was expecting him to become.

Radley kept Ben on for as long as it could – much longer than he wanted – for the brilliance, for the Oxbridge. For years, despite the guitar *and* the reading *and* the bad behaviour, he'd been unable to make his escape. Down in that vaulted cellar, with its smell of ale and underage drinkers, I wonder now what generalised hatred he must have felt to turn from the dartboard and lob his darts randomly, almost absent-mindedly, one two three, into knots of his schoolboy peers who were somehow already dead to him.

It worked; he was sent home, but I can't remember ever asking him if he was OK. He was fine. He was brilliant. Like all of us, he'd almost survived the best education in England and had an amazing career waiting just ahead of him.

Earlier that term, as editor of the magazine, he chose for the cover a photograph of a boy's face which was half mask and half face, and in his editorial he cited Orwell. Of course he did. The year was 1984, 'with all the overtones which could so easily be applied to the public school'. Orwell's dystopia had not come to pass, and Ben's staff-approved text is content with the world as it is. His piece is full of observations about what people *could* say, looking in from the outside in 1984, 'a year when the miners' dispute had reopened real or imagined sores of class distinction'. In the same year, in the south of England, the school had chosen to 'flex its financial muscles' with construction projects that show off 'affluence and advantage' that in a less enlightened society might create 'mistrust and jealousy' about a misperceived aura of 'snobbery and elitism', not to mention 'patronising condescension'. Whatever hypothetical charges he aims at the school, the official school magazine waves them away. Unfavourable views of public schools are ill-informed, Ben mumbles, and the pupils have 'more freedom of choice than ever before'.

He did his best. Ben tried to undermine his supervised editorial by enlisting the help of George Orwell: it's *1984*, people, and you shouldn't believe everything you read in official publications. But for the school it's just 1984, a year like any other, and all is well. Nothing like *1984* could happen, not in a country like ours.

9

Lessons Learned

'I don't want to be I, I want to be We.'

Mikhail Bakunin, Letter, 7 February 1870

When I was sent home myself, in December 1983, I felt my escape as a mixture of shame and pride. Then disappointment and relief, when I understood the lack of serious consequences: I too would get away with it and be welcomed back for the next term, headed for A levels and the same Oxbridge English class as Ben. There were just the two of us and we were true believers in literature, though when Ben was thrown out a second time he was barred from school premises except to sit his exams. In response we had secret lessons in my dad's Oxford office above the Magdalen Road building yard, chatting *King Lear* across the scream of rotary saws. A one-man contagion, Ben was isolated for the exam period in the Warden's house, but got drunk anyway and vomited into his guest towel, which he hid at the back of the airing cupboard. He won a scholarship to St John's College, Oxford.

Dad kept the letter the Warden sent him, in which I'm condemned and reprieved in the same short page. Behaving badly mattered, but it didn't.

> It was all the more sad, in the light of your kind letter, that I had to send Richard home early. I must confess that his calculated and underhand discourtesy to a visiting teacher who had put himself out so selflessly on behalf of the group horrified the whole of Common Room. I have told Richard what I feel about it and I simply hope that the talents he has and the success he has enjoyed this term have not gone to his head. With your usual unswerving support I am confident that we can get things right.
>
> A very happy Christmas and New Year.

On a trip to London, instead of going to a play, I'd slipped out to visit a friend who'd been expelled some time earlier. I sat on the floor of Hugh Sands's bedroom in a high-ceilinged South Kensington flat, where we amused ourselves with a bass guitar and a lump of hash and some cans of warm Harp lager. The excitement was in the transgression, not the desultory evening. It was the kicks for their own sake, and of course to horrify the whole of Common Room.

'With your usual unswerving support' – I see now how the Warden co-opted the parents as allies, reducing the chance of a rival alliance between parents and children against him and the school. As boys we were on our own, but we knew that. We'd known it for years. Like Cameron on the Queen's Eyot in the same year, I realised or decided that sustained rebellion was a tough calling and not really me. I was half at school, half trying to escape, but only because by this stage I was so uncertain about who I really was. Instead of becoming robust characters constructed from hardship and Latin, as advertised, we expended nervous energy protecting a divided self. And divided not necessarily into two pieces but three or four or more. So much of our original character was buried or hidden, in order to cope, that later in life, profiled in the newspapers, a man like Prime Minister Johnson inevitably presented as a 'confusing, seemingly contradictory figure'.

We were flexible but stubborn. Cruel but sometimes kind. George Orwell was known for his 'odd mixture of aloofness and gregariousness', but for a boarder this combination wasn't odd at all: it was a direct result of his upbringing. He could be one thing or the other, with neither characteristic having to connect to his lost true self. Orwell, like us, was the result of two distinct worlds: school and the holidays, with their conflicting emotional demands. On the night before a new term Mum grilled us steak, with home-made chips and a fried tomato. She meant well, but the very next night we had a focus for our choked-back tears. The boundary between the two worlds was just as obvious when schoolwork was assigned for the holidays. I was psychologically incapable of decoding

171

chemistry or Latin in my bedroom at home. The books might as well have dropped from the moon.

Then there was the anxiety, every new term, of wondering whether friends were still friends because of the holidays we spent not seeing pals from school. We'd go back scrubbed and uncomfortable, hoping our families hadn't changed us and we'd remember most of the rules. I sometimes said 'Dad' to a teacher, which was horrific not for the sadness but the humiliation.

Unable to escape, we adapted. Back at school we killed one self and reanimated another, until we forgot which version, if either, was authentic. To protect the tender cavities within the divided self, evasion and secrecy became a way of life, where one big truth we always needed to conceal was that we wanted and needed our mummies. To hide this shameful fact, or other shameful facts later in life, we'd do anything, like drop or bully or betray our friends as face-saving behaviour. Hardcastle, I wiped your existence from my sleeve. We told adults what they wanted to hear and expected to be loved for it, especially when we were lying – it was kind and brave not to admit to homesickness.

The inner self dived for cover, while the split personality navigated home and school, deprivation and privilege, monastic study and mindless hedonism, Roundheads and Cavaliers. Eton had survived the king deposed and the king restored, and the newer schools were built in Eton's image: we were learning the art of survival, slipping between identities, and from early on during those Sundays out we accepted inconsistencies of character: our friends had a different name at home, hidden aspects to their personality, a secret life. *Alexander*. Like a totally different person.

The boy missed by his parents wasn't the same person we knew at school. Alexander became Al became Alex became Boris. He could pick and choose, so that for the rest of his life he can be Al *and* he can be Boris. Oswald Mosley, among his friends, was known as Tom. For less colourful personalities, a David can float in and out of Dave. After an education of restricted freedoms, we preferred to keep things fluid.

The alternating current of a boarding school life – going home, coming back again – made us nimble operators between different versions of reality. The trick was to remember that everything was temporary. The other life, at home, would resume before long. But then being at home, for barely a third of the year, felt no less impermanent. Maybe nothing could be expected to last, and life needn't be taken too seriously because actions rarely had consequences that stretched beyond a term, a holiday. From early on we experienced a lack of continuity in our life stories, with responsibility always on a timer. Act in *a calculated and underhand* manner – go away, come back later and start again.

This is what our parents were getting for their money: boys with a fragmented self in an unstable reality. We were postmodernism come to life. We had our different 'I's, some more made-up than others, customised as required because we didn't have the peace or privacy to become ourselves in our own time, in our own way. At school someone always knew where we were, or where we were supposed to be (which at Radley was *never*, according to the school rules, in *the Armoury, the Steward's Yard and Buildings or the Kitchens and Servitors' Quarters*). Growing up in public we prioritised our various public-facing fronts. We developed a serviceable shifting personality, and in time we took that home with us. We took it everywhere, because it kept us safe.

This shape-shifting was more apparent in our generation than it had been previously. In addition to our divided selves, an education entrenched in the past estranged us from the present. The country was moving on but the boarding schools weren't, with their Lavatory Parades and paedophiles and early-morning walks and beatings. In boarding school time, the sixties didn't end the post-war period, not for us, in the sense that the old belief systems and daily schedules continued unaltered. What Hibbert calls the 'disturbing social unrest' of the sixties had, by the end of the seventies, in this environment made little discernible impact. The revolution was ebbing and we'd missed it. We'd heard about it, of course, and we listened to the music ten years too late, but we had no evidence that in Britain anything could genuinely change.

At the same time we were living a unique experience – we had neither a war nor the Empire to fix our fake personalities at brave and stiff-lipped. Not even our parents had fought in a war. Even the Warden had missed the war (as opposed to his predecessor Wyndham Milligan, a decorated Major in the Scots Guards). In reality, the *Commando* defiance of THE FIGHTING FEW and FIGHT OR DIE!

174

wasn't much use against instant nuclear annihilation. We didn't seem to require 'a bit of hardship' as an important lesson, yet on we went with our Empire charade (it's a book, it's a film), not convinced by a word of it. Fake selves conforming to outdated values, we reacted to hypocrisy with cynicism. We were open at all hours for irony, adopting attitudes and learning lessons we'd never forget.

Some of these even took place in the classroom. Latin and/or Ancient Greek introduced us to the rapes and adulteries of gods and the violence and madness of emperors, commemorated with relish in the green English countryside. From the Romans we discovered that being a great man doesn't mean being a good man. Classics also maintained our connection with the ruling caste – we learned by rote our declensions and conjugations from the same book Churchill was given on his first day at school in 1882, *Kennedy's Latin Primer*. Which would have been ridiculous, even in England, so in fact we had *Kennedy's Revised Latin Primer*, revised for our benefit in 1930.

To know Latin was to be reminded of our inheritance. So that for us, quoting Latin tags as an adult was a genuinely infantile act, a residue of childhood. We spent more time following the ablative and accusative adventures of Marcus and Cornelia in *Ecce Romani* (Book 1 is called *Meeting the Family*) than we did with our own families in twentieth-century Britain.

The bell rings, so we don't have time to dwell on the irony.

The next lesson is English, where we learned poems by heart of which the most adhesive was 'The Charge of the Light Brigade'. Through repetition, the riding of the six hundred became hypnotic – *Boldly they rode and well / Into the jaws of death / Into the mouth of hell* – with Alfred Lord Tennyson heroically complicit in our partial version of history. The calamity of an idiotic cavalry charge, pigeon-chested with public school exceptionalism, was glibly recruited to the cause – *Honour the charge they made! / Honour the Light Brigade / Noble six hundred!* Tennyson's Light Brigade sent us the same message as the Roman emperors – the fact of being remembered was more important than the reason.

Otherwise, during the late-1970s energy crisis, to inform ourselves about the environment we relied not on science or geography but on the medium of poetry. Stranded in the desert, eroded by implacable forces of nature, the statue in Shelley's 'Ozymandias' is a 'colossal Wreck'. So two lessons for the price of one. Firstly, don't be worried for nature, which always overcomes in the end. And secondly, with a 'sneer of cold command' the King of Kings *is* remembered, both in the desert and in this poem, however toppled he may be. Vaunting ambition will not go unrewarded.

Fortunately, like all schoolchildren, we had the rationality of maths to offer balance. Maths can't be interpreted, not at this level, and unlike in English there *is* a right answer. In maths the truth has an indisputable numeric value – wrong can't be right – and pupils are expected to show their working. Of all the subjects, it was fine to be bad at maths. Some of us didn't have the head for it, and instead of mastering long division we bodged our way to the right answer by combining multiplication with trial and error. The lesson for life was that there was always another angle. Then electronic calculators came in, and the teachers never found out who could and couldn't do sums. Bluff it, hide it, get round it. You'll be fine. That's the takeaway for the future.

The future was also Europe, and Commander Staveley's French classroom doubled up as a language lab. Sometimes we broke out the grey headsets with attached cube-shaped microphones, but instead of valuing cross-border communication we were instantly fighter pilots in the cockpits of World War II. JERRIES AHEAD! BREAK FORMATION! We couldn't take foreigners seriously, with our General de Gaulle lookalike at the front of the class raging against our deliberately gormless pronunciations. Besides, everyone in the world spoke English. Of course they did: along with our many other assumptions of superiority, we were better than Europeans and their weedy non-global languages.

At the time, with Britain considered the sick man of Europe, this disdainful attitude couldn't have been more mistaken. It was part of a belief system at odds with contemporary fact, but politics was not among our officially available school subjects. To complement our daily navigation of male hierarchies, we therefore learned our politics from the bound burgundy *Punch* magazines. Politics was something to laugh at, the cartoons making fun of plummy battles won by Old Etonians Macmillan and Hailsham against the upstart working classes. The working man had a flat cap and a fat wife and a fag in his mouth. 'You won't understand, lad. Being on t'dole for years does summat to a man.'

Punch was ideologically Tory. 'Look at any number of *Punch* during the past thirty years,' Orwell wrote, 'you will see it everywhere taken for granted that a working-class person, as such, is a figure of fun, except at odd moments when he shows signs of being too prosperous, whereupon he ceases to be a figure of fun and becomes a demon.' To laugh at class divisions was a sign of sophisticated condescension, and these were life lessons as unassailable as playing with a straight bat or the correct conjugation of *amo*. Never mind the feeling, learn by heart the grammar.

As for our elders and betters, in *Punch* the good and the great looked reassuringly familiar. They walked like us and talked like us. The old-boy plutocrats were our own, and we were proud of their work in the Mother of Parliaments. In fact no boys anywhere were readier for a surrogate mother, nor more needy for what she had to offer: in the great Offices of State, a ministerial home. At last, home: Chequers, Chevening, Dorneywood. That would make up for everything.

To reach these heights, however, it helped to have an expedient grasp of history. As Sellar and Yeatman proposed in *1066 and All That*, their 1930 comic reworking of the history of England, history 'was the cause of nowadays'. And nowadays, as understood in private boarding schools, existed at the end of a timeline of British righteousness. The British spirit was indomitable, and later could be invoked without hesitation by a public school prime minister educated in the same period as I was: the British spirit that punched out Napoleon could easily defeat a virus.

History was facts, apparently. We started with the fact of a date, which implied that further information must also be fact. Actually the history we learned was more about the feeling – the cunning of the Elizabethans, the insouciance of Sir Francis Drake, the fight-in-the-dog gutsiness of Agincourt and the Battle of Britain. As Orwell pointed out, public school patriotism isn't faked: 'they had to feel themselves true patriots, even while they plundered their countrymen'. We became patriotic to a glamorised, limited version of English history, as if introduced to Britain like foreign tourists. Which in effect we were, so detached from 96 per cent of Britain that we might as well have lived abroad. Instead, behind the thick walls of our ancient buildings, we were falsely led to believe that we embodied the country – another variation on not being ourselves.

In history, as *1066 and All That* recognised, we were Top Nation. We were special because we'd once ruled a fifth of the globe. At the same time we were eating breakfast by candlelight, besieged and outnumbered by trade unions and socialists. As the top people in the Top Nation, and thanks to the great British spirit, we could scheme to prevail either way: we were victim or vanquisher, whichever served our purposes best. We were outnumbered; we were all-powerful. The right attitude could be manoeuvred to make everything come good in the end, with Molesworth leading the rally: 'Hurrah for St George and boo to everybody else.' Private school England remained blissfully ignorant that the planet seethed with memories

179

of British crimes we'd forgotten or never acknowledged. Bad guys casting ourselves as the good guys, we fitted ourselves with a belief system that went largely unchallenged. Educationally, it was a catastrophe.

Spiritually, to compensate, we had daily chapel to put us straight. It's a rare private boarding school that doesn't tout its Christian mission. *Our Chapel forms an important centre of our life*, claims the Pinewood prospectus. *We do believe in the influence of a religious background. We attend Chapel (Church of England) in the morning and the evening as did so many of our predecessors.*

Indeed, while getting beaten, from his bent-over position Molesworth can look up at a shelf containing six volumes of commentary on the Bible. We learned to defer to the hypocrisy that Britain was a fair-minded Christian nation – *as did so many of our predecessors* – but to become effective hypocrites ourselves we needed to know the forms that virtue was expected to take. Every weekday until the age of thirteen, twice a day including Sunday, we went to chapel. After that it was once a day except Saturdays, and again on Sunday but for twice as long.

At one sermon in the Radley Chapel, on an otherwise ordinary Tuesday evening, an outside speaker came in to explain why detonating an atomic bomb above Hiroshima, causing up to 146,000 deaths, had been the right thing to do. We were in chapel, so presumably also the Christian thing to do. Mussolini used the same argument for dropping mustard gas during his Abyssinian war, which 'was really a measure of humanity, for it had the effect of saving lives'. This was the white man's burden, to make the difficult decisions.

In early 1980, the imminent move from one boarding school to the next means that my diary is full of God. He has His all-seeing eye on public school admissions. *The examiners don't choose who comes to the school; it is God. Therefore I pray that you Lord, may give me eternal faith in you for you are The Eternal.* My piety is offered in exchange for success in the scholarship exams. *I have prayed to get to the second stage and therefore this must happen.*

Such transactional fervour is explained by my circumstances. About to change schools, I felt unsettled. I trusted God to help me as God had so often helped Britain in times of need. I called on Him again when it came to my new school's end-of-term exams in June that year, and again a couple of years later for O levels. He came good two times out of three, which was encouraging if not conclusive.

Our free-floating personalities and our divided selves were always on the lookout for somewhere to land, and religion was an established refuge. As a farewell gift, every Pinewood leaver was offered either a Good News Bible or a Book of Common Prayer. I made the obvious choice, because the Good News Bible was bigger, but in another life my uncentred self might have found a friend in Jesus. This was important, because if religion failed we became vulnerable to what Hannah Arendt calls 'the monstrous immorality of ideological politics'. We knew how to disregard our own feelings, and how to reduce other people to objects. Disintegrated as individuals, exiled from home, we craved a sense of belonging. Religion had a traditional and mystical appeal similar to patriotism, which with a small tweak could be emotionally expressed as nationalism. God bless Great Britain.

We were susceptible because from an early age we'd been told we were sent away to school *for a reason*. Each and every one of us had a manifest destiny. We could pick up the thread of our heritage and become Archbishop of Canterbury, Prime Minister, Viceroy of India, or any of the other prizes that awaited our type of Englishman. Lord Protector of England. Someone had to do it, and these posts were all once available to boy-men like us, and we should bear them in mind when making subject choices for A levels. If we failed to reach the very top, then until recently Britain's global role had offered a safety valve. Hannah Arendt is specific and convincing about this:

English society was only too glad to see them depart to faraway countries, a circumstance which permitted the toleration and even the furtherance of boyhood ideals in the public school system; the colonial services took them away.

The Empire, while offering employment and spoils, also saved England from the worst excesses of boys with this peculiarly English education. Administering vast numbers of foreigners was a gig free of the constraining principle that every human life had value. Unfortunately, by the early 1980s, this outlet for the trained hardness of our hearts was no longer available. So how else, within the borders of the United Kingdom, could our traditional English belief system express itself? At first, it seemed, in exactly the way it always had.

In 1982, Britain sent a naval and military taskforce to the South Atlantic to reclaim the Falkland Islands from Argentina. War was never formally declared, but we were in the British territorial waters of the 'right thing to do'. The ten-week campaign was more of an instinct than a war, a twitching phantom limb of Britain's avenging empire.

In public schools across the country we stopped playing half-sized snooker and read the *Daily Mail*. We weren't invited to empathise with the foreign enemy (649 dead) while the British corpses (255) were a glorious sacrifice on the road to victory. To use a prime ministerial phrase, we took it on the chin. By then we had a television, accessible at weekends and for wartime news, but on the BBC the British Army had the details wrong – not only the unfamiliar SLR rifles but the missing clarity of moral purpose. The Argentinian enemy (SCHWEINHUND, GOTT IN HIMMEL) never really came into focus. A country we knew little about, except for football, had invaded some islands we hadn't heard of which we reclaimed in the name of honour, duty, history and patriotism. The public school generals and public school foreign and defence ministers justified war with a recognisably old-school vocabulary. We won, and a year later Mrs Thatcher was re-elected as prime minister with a landslide majority.

The lesson learned from the Falklands War, at the domestic polling booths, was that a futile and costly act of bravado could be political dynamite. Especially if it evoked the great British spirit. It turned out that popular sentimental nationalism spoke the same language as the public school, and had the same taste for exceptionalism. One day, for future leaders who at that time were at an attentive and impressionable age, this revelation might again come in useful.

10

The Finished Product

'"Splish-splosh, flippety-flop!" I identified already the abstracted tone with which he produced these inane jingling phrases, as if to prevent objections being made by filling up the space and time with nonsense.'

Alan Hollinghurst, *The Swimming-Pool Library*, 1988

A levels, gap year, university. The law, the army, business, journalism. Politics. The end was within sight, and for ten years the aim had been exit velocity with a built character, a traditionally constructed self. What was an English boarding school adult supposed to look like, as the finished article? In the words of Evelyn Waugh, he'd be 'a public school man. That means everything.' The type is as recognisable now as it was then, and the value is pragmatic: 'after that the social system never lets one down'.

Public school men had to be made, because left to their own devices, children spoil. Like gardens, they grow weedy. Aristotle, quoted by St Ignatius Loyola, was supposed to have said: 'Give me the child until he is seven and I will show you the man.' The English boarding schools had a slightly different take – keep the child until he's seven. Have that quality time on us. Give us the child from eight, and ten years later we'll give you back the man. Childhood was an early-career obstacle to be overcome, as were family attachments, but once our education cut in it was designed to stay with us always. It wouldn't be much of an education, or not one worth paying for, if it left no trace. It should penetrate, so that we'd never grow out of it. Or as Molesworth, unblinking, saw so clearly: 'if you do all these things you will grow up to be as good a man as yore pater tho this statement makes your mater look a bit thortful.'

Erving Goffman, never away from his desk, leans forward over clasped hands and nods his intelligent head. We were subjected to 'batch living', eating and sleeping and working in the same place. In the total institution – 'part residential community, part formal organisation' – the self could be reshaped, even if the new approved version disconnected from whatever self we came in with. 'The establishment officially expects to alter the self-regulating inner tendencies of the inmate.' The implication was that without the grip of these schools we as individuals would remain unmade and unprepared. Our natural, unhardened selves could never cope with the future stresses of contesting a by-election or trading in stocks and shares.

For ten years, to paraphrase Hannah Arendt, we were dominated in every important aspect of our lives, and experienced the action of unlimited power. We could observe how power shaped the behaviour of individuals, and in our case the most obvious result of this moulding, evident in nearly all of us, was that we now gleamed with confidence. *We will, underpinned by our Christian ethos, strive to develop values, confidence, and resilience in boys which will strengthen and prepare them for the challenges they face.* In the outside world confidence was a first line of defence, the burnished shield that deflected a great number of day-to-day inconveniences. Truly, we were made so confident in ourselves that when challenged we insisted our education counted for nothing. We didn't choose to be privately educated. It wasn't responsible for who we were.

This kind of confident, boyish operator distrusted hesitation and nuance. After *I Love* ███, the next three hardest words for us to say were *I don't know.* We valued self-assurance, which was performed at the expense of a more honest, diffident self. A show of confidence made our parents happy about money well spent on an education that put the world at our feet. If we were pretending, we did it for them. On the surface, aged eighteen, we were fine young men.

I like Paul Watkins's memoir, *Stand Before Your God*, very much indeed. My note inside the cover reminds me I bought it in 1995, to celebrate the first time I'd been on television as a writer. However, by the end of the book his conclusions betray his schooling: the illusion of confidence

187

encourages binary attitudes neither helpful nor true. About his father's death, he writes: 'I would either be crippled for life by this or I would move on.' One or the other, black or white, weak or strong. About Eton, he decides that 'whatever the path, this school made people who either loved it or hated it. There was no middle ground.'

There probably was, Paul. This way of thinking – the drama! the importance! – is Etonian in itself, amplified by the boarding school insistence on simplified rights and wrongs, and the imperative to express a confident opinion. One thing or another; a strong, well-educated character should know.

Public school confidence worked in conjunction with manners (maketh the man, at least on the outside). Courteous to everyone, the ideal schoolboy betrayed a preference for no one. Instead of thoughts and feelings we had a formula of words for every occasion, and as everyone knew, good manners cost nothing. Except they did, the right kind as recognised by the Upper Ten Thousand. They cost about £335 a term in 1975 rising to £1,328 by 1981, the last year for which I have an invoice for the fees. In an inflationary period, even the manners cost more.

For boys slower on the uptake – perhaps those in the middle ground unacknowledged by Paul Watkins – these learned responses of confidence and courtesy could settle into the blancmange of 'nice', as immortalised by public school Tim Nice-But-Dim (Swinbrook '73–'77, retake '77–'84, as confirmed in one of Harry Enfield's sketches). The habit of terribly niceness sometimes hardened like old glue, for fear of the contradictions that lay beneath,

though among ourselves we happily agreed to these eva-
sions. If I chose not to show myself as I was, then that
was fine, because my private school chums were equally
content not to look too closely. For a lifetime we could
drink Pimm's like this and meet in the Twickenham car
park like this and just like this put in a good word with the
interview panel if the opportunity arose. We were friends
for life, or for as long as the illusion held.

Manners, confidence and, for the gifted boys, a finish-
ing lacquer of self-deprecation. Deprecating a false self was
surprisingly easy, because no one felt wronged. Put them
together, and these attributes merged into the magical
quality known as charm. At its most effective, charm drew
in other people, while the charmer, not so much. At its
most cynical it was a technique, a useful mechanism for
getting our own way, however unreasonably. But I also
like Sally Rooney's description of a boy's charm as something needy, 'a begging of love from people who would
otherwise hate him'. In our case, the Hugh Grant charm
had this quality of need but also acted as an extra layer of
defence. It was how we never quite said what we meant,
or what we wanted, and so avoided exposure to emotional
risk.

In cold blood we could disguise true motives, and we
became what the writer James Lovegrove – one of the featured boys in the 1987 follow-up programme to *Public
School* – calls 'exotic reptiles'. We were the original lizard
aliens, though no one need worry we were plotting to take
over. We'd done that centuries ago, and in and around
the 1980s a fresh cohort of reptilian pseudo-adults left

their public schools equipped with a functioning false self designed by the frightened little boy they used to be. As small boys we'd dressed up as adults, in ties and polished shoes. As adults we perfected a first-class show, an excellent impression of the man we were taught to become.

By now we'd lost the ability to distinguish homesick from unsettled, confident from defended, truth from lies, and we no longer cared one way or the other. Hannah Arendt knows who we are: 'The outstanding negative quality of the totalitarian elite is that it never stops to think about the world as it really is and never compares the lies with reality.'

What did we know, by now, of the world as it really was? By the end of our schooldays it had been a while since we confronted the realities of social inequality or national status or our own personal emotional deprivation. Our experience was relabelled as an excellent education, as if those realities never existed. For years our polished boarding school selves had battled awkward truths, but the campaign had ended in victory, of a sort. *Honour the charge they made! / Honour the Light Brigade.* We were brave and had toughed out the hard times, perfected our attacks and our defences.

The beatings, the early-morning runs, the competition, the finished meals and Bible readings and prayers on our knees before bed, all of it had been good for us. Withdrawing from everyday British life was good for us. Emotional denial and coldness was good for us, as was looking down on all other lives but our own. We defied the world as it really was. *I want my mummy.* Lie.

The truth was that we needed to 'settle down', to make the most of the finest education money could buy.

It was different for earlier generations: they had their insubstantial outlines coloured in by global conflict. They were made serious by collisions with reality, despite themselves. As children and then as adults, we were not. Instead, in the anything-goes Thatcherite free market of the early eighties, we were free to indulge selves that didn't have to be serviceable to run an empire or win a war. By 1984 we were closing in on the longest ever period of peace in Europe, and Europe's political union made surpassing that record a stone-cold certainty: as individuals and as a country we weren't expecting a bump from a European world event.

In the absence of seriousness, the 1980s set a tone in which charming could become an end in itself, as could funny. Ironic. The selfish spirit of the times, for the prosperous, allowed us to perfect the strategic behaviour at which Goffman predicted we'd excel: 'an opportunistic combination of secondary adjustments, conversion, colonization, loyalty to inmate group, so that the inmate will have maximum chance, in the particular circumstances, of eventually getting out physically and psychologically undamaged'. We made the most of being two-faced or, in Goffman's words, honed our talent for making an 'opportunistic combination of secondary adjustments'.

In the novel *A Perfect Spy*, John le Carré describes the arc from boarding school upbringing to outstanding liar. True to the habits of his schooldays, though, he masks his insights behind the lie of a fiction: 'Like Rick [his father] he was learning to live on several planes at once. The art of it was to forget everything except the ground you stood on and the face you spoke from at that moment.' The face could change, because former Eton teacher le Carré knows that he and his private school contemporaries are 'entirely put together from bits of other people'. John le Carré's real name was David Cornwell. Paul Watkins now writes thrillers under the pseudonym Sam Eastland. Old Etonian Eric Arthur Blair became George Orwell, but in the list of potential pseudonyms sent to his agent he could equally have been P. S. Burton, Kenneth Miles or H. Lewis Allways. *You could get hurt very badly at a place like Eton.*

We invented and destroyed ourselves at will, a talent useful for actors, comedians, spies, politicians and writers. For the lazy, there was safety in archetypes, selves grabbed casually off the peg. The English Gentleman, for example, or John Bull, or a model of Englishness known in the seventeenth century as the 'sham good fellow'. We had him in our closets, often close to the front.

Boarding school offered an apprenticeship in charlatanism, because a false self was much easier to develop in a place without parents. In a total institution, for example, according to Erving Goffman, a boy 'learns that a defensible picture of self can be seen as something outside oneself that can be constructed, lost, and rebuilt, all with great speed and some equanimity'. Self-invention and self-promotion as a defensive/offensive skill had the happy side effect of securing privileges and prizes, and in our fluid element of half-truths and fictions we tried out different identities as readily as different names.

A provisional personality suited the extreme disconnections of boarding school: every new term we started afresh, until we came to feel entitled to regular fresh starts. As long as we were commended for being anyone but ourselves, we never genuinely matured or had to stop being boys, and we could happily alternate the English ruling-class vices of the nineteenth century – adventuring and exploitation one day, cold-heartedness and hypocrisy the next. Whatever we could get away with, whichever identity rewarded us best, with little regard for the mess we left behind. Goffman again: 'In this unserious yet oddly exaggerated moral context, building up a self or having it destroyed becomes something of a shameless game.'

Adrift from the myth of the Christian English gentleman, disappointed by the ineffectual social revolution of the sixties, undisciplined by Empire or war, boarding school boys from the 1980s were psychologically equipped to reactivate the perfidy of perfidious Albion. We could do what we wanted, without consequences, our shifty public school mindset ready-made to revive the bad reputation of the English ruling class. A reputation that existed everywhere except among ourselves. At an early age, that mindset might develop most keenly in the editor of the Eton school magazine, say, as he dabbled in power without responsibility. Or in the president of the Debating Society, where he picked up the rhetorical skills to adopt contradictory positions, once a month repeating his heartfelt declaration that 'This house believes ... ' whatever the house was believing that week.

The standard register, when speaking in public, was an amused distance that implied a superior position without having to assert it. This ironic sensibility was one manifestation of the removed self, as revealing as a changed name. Irony was a mood we inhabited and a part of what we became, and people not educated like us generally agreed that we were remote, not just from others but from ourselves.

A journalist friend of mine, who worked at the *Daily Telegraph* with Johnson, once found herself standing next to him on the platform at Canary Wharf DLR station in London. He was on his way to record a rap at Channel 4, and after practising that for an easy laugh he nudged her to agree that the whole performance was absurd, which it was. But the pretensions of the *Daily Telegraph* were also absurd. Not everyone could see this, but he could, and he charmed his colleague by assuming that she could see it too. What a joke everything was, if you knew how to look, like he looked.

Over time, in our parallel existence in a total institution, we experienced a moral loosening, one effect of 'living in a world within a world, under conditions which make it difficult to give full seriousness to either of them'. The real world wasn't serious, nor was the made-up world of school; you weren't serious and nor was I. We knew that to hurt or be hurt it was necessary to strike at the core of whatever was taken most seriously, like wanting to go home. Against which our own best defence was to take nothing seriously at all, or at least to give that impression. With enough pretending the illusion merged with reality

– it was very important to us that nothing was serious, most of all our hopelessly lost selves. *Splish-splosh, flippety-flop*. Fill up the space and time with nonsense.

Really, everything was a game, everything, and as a game life was bearable. Better, it might just become winnable.

Hannah Arendt shakes her head. Her research tells her that this game-playing liberated the English to misman-age their colonies, which for boys like us became 'a world of infinite possibilities for crimes committed in the spirit of play, for the combination of horror and laughter, that is for the full realisation of their own phantom-like exist-ence'. In a classic example of a public school half-truth, we drag fair play into almost every arena as a defining English characteristic. The play was always ours, not so much the fairness.

If in doubt, we played the game by belittling anyone and everything, new, old, true, false, beautiful, ugly. In this process the fake grown-up doing the belittling didn't grow, but if we stayed the same and everything around us looked smaller we ended up feeling the big man in any case. We became world king, without ever having to change.

11

Connections

'I must endure all, they said, for the sake of ... I have forgotten what exactly – perhaps my career.'

Robert Graves, *Goodbye to All That*, 1929

Ghosts should be easier to see while Radley College
is empty. Three or four times a week I walk into the
school, past the Lodge, and the first ghost is a blue plaque
commemorating the composer George Butterworth, a
victim of the Somme who for a year lived in this building
that now serves as the school's security hub. A curve of
black-backed monitors is visible in the bay window. On
the blue plaque Butterworth is remembered with a line
from the Housman poem he famously put to music, 'The
Lads in Their Hundreds'. *And there with the rest are the
lads that will never be old*.

In the mid-May sunshine, a heat haze shimmers above the tarmac of the long, slightly rising drive, and the flag above the memorial arches barely moves against the blue sky, as empty of high white contrails as in 1980. Normally this would be term time, and the air temperature and bird-song are at levels I recognise, as are the shape and direction of clouds at this time of year. The weather too is aligned for ghosts, and I feel a slight chill in the air between lessons and lunch, which will lift before cricket nets later in the day. The summer-term wisteria is in bloom, and the climbing roses beside the A Social housemaster's door.

I see Ben Hinchliff running along in his grey trousers tight to the hips, head buzzing with poems and keen to jump the queue for lunch. I see Hugh 'Bobby' Sands swinging his upper body left and right, gown flapping, his folders and workbooks inked with the heavy lettering for Iron Maiden and Motörhead. My friends are ghosts, and I remember every occasion since the day I left that I've spoken to a school contemporary. Three in total, in over thirty-five years, including the time I interviewed professional rugby player Chris Sheasby for *Muddied Oafs*. Apart from that last meeting, in each instance we made well-mannered small talk and moved on, untouched. The same is true of my close-knit gang at prep school, disbanded at the age of thirteen. I never saw those boys again even though I loved them. At public school, lesson learned, I was wary of deep friendships and the pattern of hurt: to love and then to leave.

Which meant I missed out on the connections for life that my dad must have envisaged, and which seem psychologically plausible as well as socially desirable: bands of boarding school brothers united by a common early bereavement and increasingly fond recollections of a ludicrous ancient history. Cameron surrounded himself with like-minded people – of the six men who worked on the Conservative Party Manifesto in 2014, five had been to Eton. The other was an old boy of St Paul's. Sonia Purnell says Johnson doesn't have friends – his younger brother was best man at his first wedding – but he knows what kind of person makes him feel comfortable. He remains loyal to boys' school boys like Guppy and Cummings, rebels but *public school* rebels. They secrete the same damage, are trapped by the same failings, and inside the fastness of English social immobility they feel secure in the continuation of the game.

Anyone who wants to join in, to avoid becoming the *custos*, better learn the rules. If you're not one of us but want to thrive, you need at the very least to recognise us for what we are. And the more like us you can be the better you'll get on, because this is England and beyond our exceptional circle the country is filled with idiots, with nincompoops and oiks and yobs. That's why in business and in the law courts, in Parliament and on procurement committees and at the tennis club, we prefer to stick together. But anyone who shares our damage for other reasons – their own troubled upbringing, their insecure sense of self – may find in us their people. For promotion and preferment, and up to a certain level neither women nor minorities are excluded, behave like a sad little man.

So do join us, if you too believe you're the best England has to offer, or have the private school instinct to pretend that this is true. The rewards may follow, if you learn our little ways. The damage trickles down, poisoning the veins of the body politic.

The only three people I really liked at public school were Bobby Sands (expelled), Ben Hinchliff (expelled) and Sally Fielding, none of whom were like the other boys. Sally has an OBE now, for services to equality in the labour market, a successful escapee because she arrived in the sixth form, wasn't a boarder and wasn't a boy. Some people have all the luck. Maybe it's too late to get back in touch, to feel for the lifelong clique that was flagged as payback for endurance, but I contact Sally anyway. She's on Twitter as CEO of the Road Safety Trust, and on Zoom one evening after working from home her friendly face pixelates easily between Sally now and the vision I have of Sally aged seventeen. I try not to do that, but even with her glasses and my greying beard, I feel we're a young pair of old people. Maybe everybody feels this way.

'What did you expect,' I ask (I've brushed my teeth), 'as the only girl going into a school of about 550 institutionalised teenage boys? Your dad was a teacher, but you can't have felt prepared.'

Sally laughs. She laughs a lot, at first. 'I was a naive sixteen-year-old and I expected to be mobbed. I'd be fending boys off. What I ended up with was complete Coventry for a term. Nobody spoke to me. The first term was absolutely horrendous.'

The head of her house eventually sat her down and explained that nobody wanted to make the first move. Sally was told that the boys were 'scared shitless, and would have the piss ripped out of them for evermore. Which explained everything.' A natural introvert, after Christmas Sally approached boys at random and talked to them. She was the one who changed the situation for the better, because years of expensive education had left the rest of us petrified, unfriendly, absent in our fantasies.

'The boys were more self-conscious than I appreciated, and more so than blokes I've met since. They were really worried about what other boys would think. But then they were terrible gossips, worse than women. I was taken aback by how quickly a rumour could spread.'

Or what these days the unattributed sources close to Number Ten prefer to think of as messaging.

Sally's older brother – a boy in the school so he too had his fixed ideas – gave her three pieces of advice. One – no more than three boyfriends over the two years or she'd be 'easy meat'. Two – walk head-high out of the dining hall because every boy would be assessing the size of her arse. Thanks, bro. Three – Sally forgets what number three was. By this time she was navigating solo.

I ask her if she keeps in touch with anyone.

'Not really. I made a conscious decision not to.'

Snap, so of course I'm pleased to hear this. I'm hoping Sally escaped unscathed because in a school that encouraged exceptionalism she was genuinely exceptional, for obvious reasons. She didn't have to end up like the rest of us, and not only because she lived with her parents and had just the two years to navigate. She says: 'I definitely chose to opt out of the network.'

'What about the influence of the school on you personally, on your personality?'

I'm thinking of the Warden's 'courteous', 'honest', 'useful' and 'confident but not arrogant', the adjectives he promised to instil whether we liked it or not.

'There was a downside for my character. It sort of made me quite hard, hard-natured. I probably ... I have a wall of defence that I quickly put up if I sense I'm being attacked in some way. I distance myself physically and emotionally. I didn't want to get hurt at Radley, and that was my defence mechanism.'

The school did what the school does, whoever you are. For me, Sally was a ray of light, and undoubtedly she represented a sense of escape, or possibility. There was a limit, however, to the impact she could have. John Dancy was the Marlborough College headmaster who opened up his sixth form to girls in 1968 (the school is now fully co-educational). 'Marlborough remains a boys' school,' he said. 'I am convinced it's a much better boys' school for having some girls in it.'

And Radley in 1982 was a better school for having even one girl in it. I have a final question.

'Did you marry a public school old boy?'

'No!' On the screen Sally throws back her head, and thank God she's laughing again. 'Definitely not! No I didn't!'

Up at the school, past the buildings, through the golf course, I smell nettles and damp cow parsley and stroll with the ghost of Sally Fielding. Even in *1984*, in the months of May and June, Winston and Julia couldn't help but fall in love. I want to smoke a cigarette, though I haven't smoked for twenty years, feeling melancholy with the living past, the living dead. On these walks I'm a ghost myself, or part-ghost, inhabited by my former boyhood self, and now we've come this close together I wonder what to do with him. Orwell warns that 'whoever writes about his childhood must beware of exaggeration and self-pity', a statement in which I hear his boarding school distrust of feeling: a common self-sabotage is to dismiss every emotion, whatever it may be, as self-pity.

'Are you OK?'

My younger boy-self tells me he's fine. Really, school wasn't that bad. He expects he'll settle down pretty soon.

I touch the gatepost near the beagle kennels which marks the turning point of the footpath's up and back. Back down through the avenue of beech trees, up again towards the classrooms and on the left is the Bigside cricket pavilion. He was fine and I was fine. Of course we were, because I slept in this place for years for my own good. I was fortunate and privileged to be here. I was not sad or miserable or homesick.

As I walk I take the boy's hand and ask him again how he feels. 'You're not really fine, are you?'

'Angry.'

'Yes. I worked that one out. I can help. I've learned a lot of new words.'

I've begun to feel that I live in the village for a reason: I've come back to stage a rescue. The school up the road had taken a boy hostage, many years ago, but after some initial suspicion he's glad to see me.

'Honestly, we can do this together. It's OK.' I squeeze his hand. 'How do you feel about me being here now?'

'Good, I think. A bit frightened for you, but better. Thank you.'

We hold hands past the red-brick classrooms, past the entrance to the house where we used to live. My housemaster is dead now. He was a lovely man; I don't think we ever won a cup at anything. The Warden is dead (long live the Warden). In the memorial edition of the school magazine, from 2019, he gets a glowing end-of-life report: 'a strong emphasis on the fundamental decencies of life: behaviour, manners, unselfishness, awareness of other people'. All the other teachers from that time might as well be dead, because after thirty-five years none of the staff from 1984 can still be working here. They just drift around my psyche, all alive, internalised as different ways of criticising my instincts. I smile at them. They can't touch me, as long as I stay on the path.

'Maybe we should go there?' I've stopped walking to look at a small wooden hut about two-thirds of the way across the vast expanse of mown cricket pitches, backed by a copse of five or six leafy trees. 'For old times' sake.'

The hut is not on the public footpath and the direct route across the pitches offers no cover for a trespasser. If I were accosted I'd have to explain who I was and what I was doing. Or lie. I don't want to do those things. If I were prime minister, I'd just stride across and go where I wanted – everyone would know who I was, and I could do whatever I liked.

I see the current Warden cutting across the grass from the Armoury back towards Shop. There goes my heart again. I imagine that with his unlimited power he could ruin my book. He could *punish* me, which as a feeling is both real and ridiculous. I checked on Wikipedia, and the Warden is four years younger than I am, which helps. I intersect his route and when he crosses the public footpath I say hello. I introduce myself. So as not to be threatening I take a step towards him and hold out my hand. He recoils, arms in the air, as instantly in horror do I. Neither of us wants to infect the other.

Gesturing with a straight palm – it would be rude to point – I say I'd quite like to go to the wooden pavilion in the middle of the pitches. His reply is equivocal. I can, but I can't. I can't, but I can.

'It doesn't have to be now,' I say, 'but if anyone stops me can I say that we spoke about it?'

'I'd rather you didn't.'

The message I get is that I can go there, but not with his permission, and not while he's watching on. That feels about right. That's a solution that I and my younger self can understand. I thank him and wish him luck in these strange times, when no one knows for sure if our leaders – educated in a school like this one – can be trusted to save our lives. As the Warden walks away I reach out to my side, feeling for the best of what remains of me. Too late. The moment has passed us by.

We were educated to succeed, and conventional success stories resolve themselves in the usual places. I have school contemporaries among the captains of industry and the Parliamentary Under Secretaries of State and the partners of corporate law firms. Also in the news, though some time ago now, two brothers who murdered their parents with a Chinese rice flail, before dismembering and burying the bodies. It can go more than one way.

In the early eighties success or failure was initially judged by A-level results, as an immediate verdict on whether the parents had received value for money. The school therefore talked up its percentage of A and B grades, along with successful Oxbridge applicants. At around this time an article in the *Eton Chronicle* has figures showing that about a third of Eton leavers went to Oxford or Cambridge Universities. Individually, these boys no doubt shone with confidence, as I did. We were arrogant, brittle, well read and fearless, but it was ludicrous to judge our education on how we were at seventeen and eighteen. These schools know our percentage of As and Bs at A level, but have no idea of our percentage of Fs and Us at life. We ought to undergo assessments at thirty years old, forty, fifty, fifty-three, fifty-five, at whatever age the prime minister is now. Anyone can keep cut flowers handsome for a day.

The *Update* documentary that follows on from *Public School* sets out to address this issue. In 1987, eight years after the filming of the original programme, the square-jawed Dennis Silk is still enthroned as Warden, and as in the original series he is 'uneasy in his part'. In the opinion of Christopher Hibbert, the Warden gave 'an impression of ingratiating unctuousness instead of sincerity and understanding in dealing with boys', and these characteristics are again evident in his lengthy on-camera answer to the 'girl question'. The answer to the question (except for teachers' daughters, who in most cases are understandably reluctant) is no.

By 1987 nothing much at the school has changed, while the boys filmed in 1979 are now older and interviewed at university or at work. In their twenties it's too soon to call them successes or failures. Intensely guarded, they congratulate themselves on their 'mature personalities', cautiously optimistic that their education did them more good than harm. Asked about the original programme, they say what can you do, when watching it back, except laugh?

Which must bug a younger documentary-maker, Hannah Berryman, who gets a second update off the ground in 2013, called *A Very English Education*. If I did have friends from school, this is how they'd be thirty years later, and no one's laughing now.

As middle-aged men, these boys make for a desperately sad film. A commodity broker, single in his late forties and living in Hong Kong, has savings to cover the private education of the children he doesn't have. Two of the other old boys have emigrated to Australia, and both are trying to break their regrettable inheritance of 'not a physically affectionate household', and 'not a very touchy-feely expressive family'. The best interviewee is sportsman and scholar Donald Payne (he came first in a class of five boys) who hated always having to be the best, so much so that at home in Perth with his loving family he breaks down in tears. To close the documentary Berryman takes him back to the school, and films him against a background of the red-brick chapel on a summer's day. The last line of the film is from Donald, more in hope than anger: 'In the end, it's just school.'

If it was just school, no one would pay so much money.

'It's a club,' says another of the ageing boys. Maybe, but cancelling membership is less straightforward than fleeing to the other side of the planet. The most troubling character, in both updates, is the most obvious success – army officer to investment banker, with an office in Chelsea name-taped in brass. He accepts that the right kind of school is 'essential for what I'm doing now', whereas state schools fail because of 'a poverty of ambition'. He has no sympathy.

I'd like to know soft-eyed Donald (Dr Payne) as a friend, but not this other man, even though friendships calibrated like hedge funds can be the secret of English success. Public school friends come in useful. When he was Brussels correspondent for the *Daily Telegraph*, for example, Johnson claimed he 'was acting out of loyalty to an old friend' when he agreed to help locate a fellow journalist so his pal could have him physically assaulted. The 'old friend' was from school, of course he was, and the targeted journalist was not one of them ('these people are … it's like they're like dogs'). Johnson's educational heritage features strongly in the recorded phone call at the centre of his Guppygate episode. Black eyes and a cracked rib can be dismissed as a joke – 'Nothing which you didn't suffer in rugby, OK?' Tellingly, Johnson signs off with a promise – 'OK, Darry, I've said I'll do it. I'll do it, don't worry.' No one knows whether he did or not. Truth, lies, who's to say?

By the time the Guppy tape surfaced Johnson was Mayor of London. He was a success, making the most of his head start in life, but already his loyalty to people like us looked like a decidedly mixed blessing. Later, when another of the boys' school boys tested everyone's eyesight with some lockdown driving to Barnard Castle, Johnson again placed loyalty ahead of integrity or decency. At least for a while. Once he and Cummings fell out, each was right to be frightened of the other. Their schooling was more powerful in them than any self-projection as maverick or rebel: they knew how to hurt their own.

As high-flying successes we could evidently fail as human beings, though we rarely saw this for ourselves. In our estimation of success and failure, we tended to visions of exceptionalist extremes: prime minister or 'tramp dread'. I first came across this phrase in Martin Amis's memoir *Experience*. A committed public school boy didn't entertain the possibility of failing into mediocrity – only pissing into his trousers outside a Tesco would do. There is glamour, for a boy who believes he's special, in being down and out in Paris and London. For me, less steeped in the tradition, I had 'provincial prep-school teacher dread'. An utter failure, I'd live in a single room across from the top of the main staircase, my meagre success measured in absolute power over terrified children: 'You boy! Come here at once!'

The worst didn't happen – I'm neither back at school nor prime minister. I bailed out early, I think. In the 1980 diary there's an unusually outward-looking passage that wonders why Presidents Kennedy and Lincoln didn't keep their itineraries a secret. *If you declare everything you do you*

will in some way be mentally assassinated. Do you want this?
I did not. Better to stay in the shadows, making caution
and secrecy a way of life. I was too circumspect for prime
minister, never quite believing that I was exempt from disaster because my parents had paid for my schooling. My
brother died. I pulled my neck in.

Thankyou Lord for my 12th year that I have survived it.

Some boys did go off the rails. Bored of the odds in
their favour, public school boys could go looking for bad
luck, to make a change. Others were derailed by the logic:
they wanted to commit the crime that fitted the punishment. If our parents didn't want us at home we must have
done something wrong. In which case, we'd *prove* there
was something wrong with us. Drugs and drink were available and ultimately, if we were serious, the street. Watch
this space, this empty space where a functioning adult self
should be.

I weigh up this equation whenever I read about an
inherited fortune squandered, including those from centuries before our own. These grandiose failures can be
read as successes, stories of emphatic revenge for having
been left as a child in the care of strangers. Other failures,
like the schoolmaster Grimes in Waugh's *Decline and Fall*,
end up facing the lowest moment of all: 'I sat there for
some time looking at that revolver. I put it up to my head
twice, but each time I brought it down again. "Public-
school men don't end like this," I said to myself.'

Public-school men are expected to know better.

*

At first, every pathway appeared open. We had the confidence and the money. We had the education. And beyond the end of Empire, we could contemplate routes to influence and power that were a lot more fun than colonial administration, like writing novels and journalism.

Most public school boys possess Orwell's first attribute to qualify as a writer, as set out in his essay 'Why I Write':

> 1. Sheer egoism. Desire to seem clever, to be talked about, to be remembered after death, to get your own back on grown-ups who snubbed you in childhood, etc., etc. It is humbug to pretend this is not a motive, and a strong one.

Orwell never lost touch with the language, the *humbug*, so he'd have known that another perk of privilege is the transience of failure. If we have the habit of falling on our feet, it's half because we have the habit of falling: Johnson wrote a largely forgotten novel called *Seventy Two Virgins*. Try something else. Fail again. Try journalism, try politics, fool more of the people more of the time. Success didn't require original manoeuvres, only a repeat of what boys like us habitually did to succeed. It helped that ambition was essentially a confidence trick, and a socially acceptable method to outrun a damaged self. If other people got hurt along the way, or left behind, then we'd learned early to look out for ourselves. We didn't rely on other people, and they shouldn't rely on us.

The rewards for conforming to the total institution, according to Goffman, were release with an 'honourable discharge' and a 'personal recommendation'. In his gap year between school and university, David Cameron was given an internship at the House of Commons by his godfather. Johnson didn't have the same finger-click connections, but in the words of Evelyn Waugh he was now 'a public-school man. That means everything.' The system wouldn't let him down, and it didn't: the luck of the caste had him spending his year at Geelong Grammar School, the 'Eton of Australia'. Right from the start he wasn't let down, and nor was I when after university I was employed without experience or qualifications as a schoolmaster. I knew how to format the letter, and how to play the game. Inky knew where I'd been, and trusted me to charm the parents.

And if it didn't work out, which it didn't, I'd left a back door open. If trouble came in at the front, we knew how to slip out the side. We made sure always to pull up short of the point of no return, careful not to expose ourselves by committing to fixed principles or convictions. This was either smart or the lifetime farce of unlimited reinvention, depending on your point of view. From our POV, it was all good. We strategised, we manoeuvred: that was our educational advantage.

Unless we lost the knack.

When I was a constituent in Wells, with young children, the Conservative MP sent out a campaign leaflet with his politically happy family pictured on the front. I therefore felt justified in asking his position on the funding of local schools, and whether his children made use of them. His agent told me that the MP's children were 'at school in London' to be closer to their father's place of work – meaning the House of Commons. His sons, I already knew, were at Eton. I recognised the characteristic half-truth, the manoeuvring and the exceptionalism, and I had little sympathy until I read, later, that after leaving Eton one of his sons had travelled to the family hunting lodge in Scotland and shot himself. These schools didn't work for everybody.

On the internet I search for my expelled friend Hugh Sands, but the little information I have – his school, his home address from forty years ago, his schoolboy interests – isn't enough to track him down. I can find no sign of him. Perhaps he succeeded in escaping.

Nor did I keep in touch with Ben Hinchliff, not after those Oxbridge exams, because I didn't keep in touch with anyone. From Cambridge onwards I didn't think about him for years. I heard, I don't know from where, that at Oxford he'd given up English for Law, and then trained as a barrister. It made sense. Barrister was a lucrative outlet for literary ability and a gift of the gab. Of course he was brilliant at law, too, beating them in the Temple at their own game. Then later again he decided the only reality was in the land, and he'd gone back to Yorkshire to run the family farm.

It sounded to me like Ben was a success on his own terms, doing his thing, being his own man. He'd found a way out. *If we are all to grow up like that wot is the use of going on, eh?* He wasn't like the rest of us. He was fine. I found a great press photo of him in his days as a barrister in London, striding away from a victory in court, tie and wig off, fag in hand, job done.

But I went down rabbit holes looking for pictures as a diversion from the first-up search results. On Google, before all else, Ben was a newspaper headline.

FORMER BARRISTER FOUND DEAD THREE WEEKS AFTER WEDDING.

In November 2013, aged forty-six – close to the same age as Prime Minister Cameron and three years younger than Johnson the Mayor of London – Ben was married in a ceremony close to his family farm near Sheffield. Three weeks on from the wedding, after returning from the honeymoon, he went to a storage area above the garage on his farm, where he was later 'found dead from a single gunshot wound'. Ben Hinchliff was a human interest casualty in the *Daily Mail* and the *Daily Telegraph*, and in all the Yorkshire papers.

In my memory he's a sixteen-year-old English literature genius with a liking for the Rolling Stones and a habit of running down corridors without bending his knees. He wears his trousers low and tight on his hips, without a belt. He's the Ben of *King Lear* in my dad's office above the building yard, and for years whenever I was in St Giles I'd check the gates of St John's College, just in case. I once saw Seamus Heaney out on the pavement, waiting for a taxi.

'"Public-school men don't end like this," I said to myself.' That's how Grimes walked away: suicide wasn't for us. Ben had tried out success, as a high-flying barrister, but fulfilling the expectations of his education had turned out to be no success at all. He'd done what they hadn't wanted and then what they had, and still his inner being wouldn't

rest. So he threw it all away, like a public school spy for the Soviet Union. He hated what he'd become. He escaped, he tunnelled out.

The wife of his farm manager told the *Daily Mail*: 'He always had a smile on his face, was always very friendly which is why all this has come as a huge shock. In short he was a lovely man.'

His chambers in London set up a JustGiving page and raised £2,270, which they donated to the Charlie Waller Memorial Trust, a charity founded after the suicide of Old Radleian Charlie Waller in 1997, at the age of twenty-eight. Charlie's friend the TV presenter Mark Durden-Smith said: 'You'd have thought he had everything.'

12

Success/Failure

'At that time failure seemed to me to be the only virtue. Every suspicion of self-advancement, even to "succeed" in life to the extent of making a few hundreds a year, seemed to me spiritually ugly, a species of bullying.'

George Orwell, *The Road to Wigan Pier*, 1937

R un with the overdogs. Keep those awkward feelings inhibited and never look back. You'd have thought we had everything, so we hit the ground running and during the posh boy eighties we made the most of our advantages in the Temple and the City and at Westminster. This was both a fulfilment of educational promise, and not. 'Clearly there was only one escape for them,' says Orwell in the 1940s of his former schoolmates, '– into stupidity.

They could keep society in its existing shape only by being unable to grasp that any improvement was possible.'

We made an unconscious promise to our parents to succeed, which justified the break-up of the family and the financial hit. From the first evening at school aged eight we promised not to cause trouble and to be brave little soldiers. We'd done that. Now we had to demonstrate that what we'd done had been the right thing to do. We might even become obsessed with this 'right thing', even if we had no coherent notion of what it was. Cameron is 'right' four times in the first two pages of *For the Record*. Elsewhere the Brexit referendum was his right thing to do, and air strikes on Syria were the right thing to do, and walking away leaving Parliament to sort out the mess was the right thing to do. There are YouTube compilations that lose track of how many 'right things to do' Cameron did. He's so fixated on being right, I worry for how secretly wrong he must feel.

The 'successful' among us did the right thing from morning through to night, and conveniently England was arranged in such a way that 'the right thing to do' was usually in our own best interests. Of course it was. We arranged it. Our education custom-equipped us to nurture and sustain our specific Tory inheritance, and 'the construction of a coherent tribe was the true business of the schools; a self-perpetuating, hierarchical system where the means of advancement was bound up with obedience, respect for tradition and one's seniors'. So says Alex Renton in *Stiff Upper Lip*. The right habits for life included feeling driven towards making a success of ourselves, with old school values determining the lifestyle that counted as success.

Yet keeping your top button done up and developing a manic work ethic could grow into a form of cowardice, an excuse for not having to look life in the eye. Overworking was easier than self-reflection, making success another way of not having to deal with the realities of life, like failure. The downforce of emotional repression could be offset by a bounce-back of professional ambition, and we were encouraged from an early age to ask ourselves how far we could go. How much reach could we put between the outer buffer of the man and the inner softness of the child? We were taught to keep moving forward, excellent advice for a boy on the run, and the rewards are apparent in the digitised school magazines.

Radley College Gazette

_____ was appointed as Minister of State for Trade Policy at the Department for International Trade. Previously he served as the Prime Minister's Parliamentary Private Secretary from July 2016 to June 2018.

_____ has this year finished his appointment as High Commissioner to New Zealand, after which he was Principal Private Secretary to the Secretary of State for Foreign and Commonwealth Affairs under Boris Johnson's tenure.

'Driven' was the demon we liked to name, but despite our many privileges we don't get to name our own demons, or they end up looking like qualities we quite admire. The genuine demons were nastier, and they fed and bred in the gap between who we pretended to be and who we actually were. We gave over to them the freedom of a wide territory, and instead of looking ahead we'd have been wise to look behind, look back, see the demons from our schooldays in pursuit.

Except we were usually too busy – ambition was more acceptable than suicide as a way of deadening the self. Get elected president of the debating society. Edit the school magazine. Lobby to become head of house, head prefect. Join a milkround company, get a column on a national newspaper, write a book. For the worst afflicted, at the high end of the greasy pole, become prime minister. The classic markers of success were picked off greedily by those most terrorised by failure.

In that sense, the conformists were the casualties, end-lessly fulfilling their unconscious promise to their parents not to fail or get into trouble. The drive for success was an unresolved and ongoing plea for attention and affec-tion, a condition described by Lucille Iremonger in 1970 as the Phaeton complex. In Greek mythology Phaeton was a frustrated child of the sun god Helios, who insists on driving his father's chariot just for one day. He crashes the chariot, turning much of Africa into desert.

According to Iremonger, a hunger for power is the tragic fate of children abandoned by their parents, and she devel-oped her theory from a study of British prime ministers between 1809 and 1940. No prizes for guessing where most of them were educated, and many successful former boarders can be recognised as Phaetons. Immature, insecure, we suf-fered a 'traumatic and unusual experience' in childhood that transformed into ferocious ambition in later life. Phaeton's blind sense of purpose, Iremonger notes, 'could lead only to disaster for himself, and possibly for others'.

But in our contrary and blinkered world, disasters could be recorded as successes. In the twentieth century, public school boys were fascinated by the Victoria Cross, Britain's highest decoration for valour. Churchill's best friend Milbanke was killed in the Gallipoli campaign at Suvla Bay, a fiasco often blamed on Churchill himself, but the VC won earlier in South Africa made Milbanke's life a triumph. A medal was available for anyone like Tony Money who had 'a complete disregard for his own life', who could be as emotionally Victorian as possible, and this kind of success, once achieved, justified and erased what had come before.

Molesworth, of course, finds time to satirise the lower-case 'v.c', awarding it to Fotherington-Thomas for 'shooting down 99 spaceships of mars'. Medal pinned to his chest, Fotherington-T then gets himself killed in action. Ultimately, however, despite or because of his cynicism, Molesworth can't escape his education. In his final diary entry he signs off with a last-minute dream of conventional success:

But I do not think I will ever be the BRANE of BRITAIN as every other boy will be. Perhaps by that time there will be room in the world for a huge lout with o brains. In which case I mite still get a knighthood.

THE END

Don't worry, Nigel, England traditionally reserves places at the top table for louts with o brains. Molesworth's sudden yearning for establishment glory may well be satisfied: at school he has learned nothing, he has learned everything. Thanks to St Custard's he can plausibly eye up a knighthood.

In *The Old Boys*, David Turner has the statistics for the 'highly disproportionate share' of public school alumni in the top jobs of the United Kingdom. These figures come from 2014, to include boys at school at the same time as me in their middle-aged professional prime: 'seven in ten senior judges, six in ten senior officers in the armed forces, and more than half the permanent secretaries, senior diplomats and leading media figures'. Perversely, Turner concludes that these numbers show the breadth of public school talent. A follow-up report by the Sutton Trust and Social Mobility Commission, *Elitist Britain 2019*, paints a mostly unchanged picture. Private schools account for nearly 70 per cent of the judges and barristers in the country. If there was ever any doubt, we *are* the law. To this list can be added over 50 per cent of bishops and ministers of state and lord lieutenants and the England cricket team, these doors not even half open to anyone else.

For every success story the Warden's triumphalist 1979 letter to the parents assumes a single political affiliation: 'Fortified by the great Tory victory in May we now look to the problems of the future.' The public schools were an in-house education system for the Conservative Party, never knowingly in touch with progressive ideas. In the early eighties the Oxbridge colleges, for example, are causing concern, 'as more and more Colleges go co-residential and the chances for boys decrease'. Those poor public school boys, and their uniquely diminishing opportunities. The Warden frequently cajoles the parents to fight on the right side: 'The future of Independent Schools is more fiercely than ever under threat from hostile political interests.' So give more money, join the old school Radleian Society, welcome to the barricades.

They fought and they won. We won.

Winners are easy to trace, because eminence in the twenty-first century can be spectated on the internet. I can find middle-aged contemporaries in the glow of their evident success, often in snapshots of glittery dinners at the Drapers' Hall or the Honourable Artillery Company. They're out there thriving in wood-panelled rooms that feel like home to us, meaning they feel like school. Another generation on, successful private school parents still measure their success by the ability to send their children to private school, which is for the best. Maybe the same school but maybe not, to avoid that nagging sense of lifelong damage. Anyway, everyone can see that these schools have changed now. They aren't what they were in our day.

Or maybe they are. The most recent fly-on-the-wall documentary in the tradition of *Public School* is a Cutting Edge film broadcast in 2010 called *Leaving Home at Eight Years Old*. The camera follows four girls in their first term at a Hampshire prep school (manor house, grounds, the full lunatic asylum) and the images are recognisable and sad and hollow with the familiar acres of dread. 'Mummy's silly, isn't she?' says a crying mum. 'You know why I'm crying? Because I'm happy.'

221

As entertainment, I can't say I enjoy watching small children weep. 'If we could pop them a pill every night to cure their homesickness,' the headmistress says, 'we would.' The new boarders 'just have to learn to cope', and one of the girls has a ten-year-old brother who is coping by wrapping up his face in a T-shirt.

'Why are you dressed like that?' his housemaster asks.

'We're Taliban. We're going to blow the place up.'

At least they've moved on from the Second World War.

The four girls get better at hiding their feelings, and by the end of the first term the parents judge boarding school a 'resounding success'. Every three minutes or so the YouTube video freezes and cuts to an advert. The first commercial break is for Radley College, whether by coincidence or algorithm I can't know, but Radley buys advertising space that punctuates harrowing boarding school documentaries, confirming that social outcomes remain mostly what matters. In the ad the Radley facilities are flaunted by drone, along with the collar-and-tie availability of the staff, and the rehearsal interviews for Oxford (twenty-eight prime ministers). Step onto the moving walkway towards success, step on and then walk fast in any case. England is as England was.

Our drive towards success – beyond the baubles and the social cover a successful career provides – was behaviour compelled by the silenced child inside. Success would be the elusive time we got everything we wanted, world without end, holidays without terms, home without school, amen. Success opened a gate into a safe space where as high achievers we'd exist beyond reproach, and beyond punishment. We could do what we liked, and never be caught. Sadly, with the gate locked behind us, home wasn't any closer. However successful we became, we were doomed to the failure of too late. It was always too late to turn back now.

For us, success came at a price, most commonly a fucked-up personal life. Evasive, emotionally detached, competitive; none of these classic boarding school hang-ups stood in the way of becoming a Queen's Counsel. In relationships, however, they conferred less of an advantage, and Nick Duffell's psychological profile in his book *The Making of Them* has us pinned. The successful boarding school boys are as likely as the failures to be 'exiled from their emotional vitality and internally dominated by the need to stay in control'. That was us all right: we knew not to trust in love, especially with women who claimed to love us back. Once we may have believed that, but then the cars drove away.

Equally problematic, when it came to adult relationships, was that our apprenticeship in male privilege included the lesson that girls were inferior and distracting. Duffell again, as the designated expert: 'the boarding school experience has the effect of encouraging all the worst features of male sexuality: detachment, obsessionality, idealising and devaluing women, and eventual misogyny'. Inexperienced, cloistered, we later endowed idealised girlfriends with qualities they didn't have, and couldn't possibly have, and then in time despised them for not having them. These failings were hardly surprising, really, because our exposure to homesickness had taught us to think it a failure to feel attached to an adult we loved. Women did well to be wary of successful Englishmen.

We could fuck up sex. As adults, greedy for the human contact we'd missed as children, we could substitute physical gratification for emotional intimacy. Then when a deeper intimate connection eluded or confused us, out of habit we blamed anyone but ourselves – after the initial thrill of a competitive victory we could stumble through relationships in a state of continuous low-level exasperation. Women were frustrating because they were irrational and unmade, like children. They weren't *schooled*.

We were no strangers to divorce, as demonstrated by Professor Leonard's research into education and gender. We kept a back door open – when trouble came in the front we slipped out the side.

Occasionally as husbands and fathers our defences and pretences might find a way to keep a relationship together. After a successful career, the children grown up and the grandchildren listed for a decent school, we could finally relax into corduroy trousers, drinking lunchtime G&Ts and turning down the heating. Thinking of my own dad's life, there might be a vanishing point towards the end when we had so little of our real selves in the game that we simply lost interest. We stopped being bothered about anything much, and a marriage could be kept intact by remembering that unhappy women were a major inconvenience. For the sake of an easy life, like at school, we could revive our habits of unengaged compliance. These days too would pass. The core loneliness went unchallenged, and by the end we neither reached for the dark places nor wanted to try, almost as if a long time ago in a dormitory bed we'd been there before.

Tired of psychological stratagems, of relentless ambition and the constant remaking of the unmade self, most of us with our money could relax into a vague idleness, doing no harm. Light of touch, we took nothing too seriously, in the manner to which we were accustomed. Success or failure, the result was the same, as T. C. Worsley writes of his father: 'He could, at any time in these years, have had anything he wanted, if only he had wanted anything.' He was neither a failure nor a success, the prime minister or a tramp: Worsley's father was Dean of Llandaff Cathedral. Worsley blames the caste: 'Was he asphyxiated by the responsibility that we all represented, if only in the form of guilt for never having shouldered it?'

Dying of oxygen asphyxiation, by preference in a slowly depressurising Lear jet, strikes me as among the most peaceful ways for a human being to end their days. A feeling of mild exaltation followed by apathy and unconsciousness. Comfortable in a plush seat, far above the enervating surface of the earth, we might fade towards oblivion in comfort. Stay calm and don't make a fuss about nothing, because to be awake and unhappy would betray the habits of a lifetime. Who among us *dared* to be unhappy? That wasn't who we were taught to be. Towards the end it was possible – as if privilege had a narcotic effect – to drift, to become pleasantly selfish, not even very scared of dying. Death would feel like going back to school. Not nice, not what we wanted, but we knew we'd soon get used to it.

13

Bad Little Men

'The only thing when you look at the cuning vilaninous faces in our class you wonder if history may not soon be worse than ever.'

Geoffrey Willans, *Down with Skool*, 1953

To fail by succeeding meant blundering on, shouldering others aside like an oafish adult playing rugby with children. We knew the game wasn't serious, but we still went hard. That well-worn pathway to Number Ten wouldn't walk itself.

We had no idea of our limitations. Clever boys let loose on the early eighties, we could ride a Tory wave learning nothing much more than the lessons we were taught at school. In the manner of Simon Ward as Young Winston, *you lie, you shirk, you boast, you care for nothing but yourself.*

Or as Anthony Hopkins as Lloyd George says to him in the same film: 'You're a child of your class, and you may never outgrow it.' This is the Churchill we knew from repeated viewings of the rented three-reel film – a hero, a role model, a revered ancestral spirit.

According to Sonia Purnell in *Just Boris*, Ashdown House played a 'large part' in forming the person Johnson would later become, and the school was 'one of the few subjects on which he became serious'. Boys like us were uniquely ill-suited to modern leadership yet we got to be the leaders, and schools like Ashdown were responsible for both those facts. If there was any secret to our 'success', back at school was where to look for it.

Personally, as a man of prime ministerial background and age, I'm grateful I'm not in charge. That's because I'm not surprised by the mess that people like me can make. I still think, as I did in 1979, that anyone with inside exposure to the British ruling caste will smell the rot at its core. And when public school politicians pose as populists and radicals, the fraudulence is close to absurd. In government, it's worth remembering, most Conservative innovations serve to enhance the authority of those in power rather than extend liberties to others. Tory politicians radicalise in the spirit of Lord Byron and other Harrovian prefects in the early 1800s, who fomented rebellion to preserve their right to flog junior boys.

We're as fake at radicalism as at everything else, and I wait for the electorate to denounce our imposture. I have hope, as I did in 1979, that the long English scam will soon be over. I was wrong then, too.

How bad could it get? 'English Fascism, when it arrives,' Orwell wrote, 'is likely to be of a sedate and subtle kind (presumably, at any rate at first, it won't be *called* Fascism.)' An overgrown schoolboy with his fist in his palm would deny any intention of becoming the national headmaster. What a joke! But if an English private school boy as dictator sounds far-fetched, then historically in Europe a tyrant's first steps often seem implausible, which partly explains why they weren't stopped sooner. In his 1995 essay 'Ur-Fascism', Umberto Eco repeats Orwell's warning: 'it would be much easier, for us, if there appeared on the world scene somebody saying "I want to reopen Auschwitz, I want the Black Shirts to parade again in Italian squares." Life is not that simple. Ur-Fascism can come back under the most innocent of disguises.'

We grew up entertained by the idea of tyranny. The Warden was relaxed about participants in the 1979 hustings mocking the idea of civil rights: 'I have a dream of a white Britain.' This is a speech that really happened, filmed by the BBC and accessible on YouTube (*Public School*, episode 3). Though of course it was a joke. Four years later in 1983 another joke candidate stood for the British Union of Fascists. It was a laugh, but the joke never got old, and some gags were funnier than others: the fun Socialist Workers Party candidate was booed and egged. The National Front speaker was cheered as lustily as the Tory, which taught us all a lesson. If we could play at fascism and be applauded, in politics we could play at anything.

In their defence, these boyish right-wingers were attention-seekers, but attention-seeking was another of our weaknesses. Fame and acclaim was like being loved by everyone, all the time, especially by people we didn't know and would never meet. The seeking spoke of serious defects in the history of love we'd experienced closer to home, but the attention went some way to making amends. Everyone pays attention to a world king, to a strongman leader.

Towards the end of the Second World War, during the planning stage of the most celebrated totalitarian novel in the English language, George Orwell chose to review the biography of a little-known public school headmaster, William Sewell of Radley, who 'was responsible for giving the public schools their present character'. And in 1947, only two years before 1984 was published, he sent his editor a lengthy account of his experiences at prep school. Orwell's biographer describes the essay 'Such, Such Were the Joys' as 'so unhappy and so horrific a picture of institutional despotism' that some critics have seen in it the origin of the novel.

St Cyprian's and Airstrip One, as Britain is renamed in 1984, have their similarities. In the novel, Winston Smith can't remember much of his childhood and both his parents disappeared when he was 'ten or eleven years old'. 'Seven or eight' might have seemed too cruel. 'To dissemble your feelings, to control your face, to do what everyone else was doing, was an instinctive reaction.' In Oceania, the superstate of which Airstrip One is a province, the ruling Inner Party represents about 2 per cent of the population and 'the terrible thing that the Party had done was to persuade you that mere impulses, mere feelings, were of no account'. The torturer O'Brien has a 'schoolmasterish manner', the food is terrible and as at boarding school everyone will be happier when the orgasm is abolished.

At Eton, George Orwell was taught French by Aldous Huxley, two Etonian writers who between them mapped the dystopian spectrum in twentieth-century English literature. Their experience of school was the formative influence they shared. A boys' boarding school could grow the fictional Big Brother and also the Controller in *Brave New World*, who according to SparkNotes (so shoot me: we're not at school now) represents a society 'where conformity and stability are more valued than emotion and individual freedom'. You could make this stuff up, with the right childhood experiences, but could the English boarding schools ever produce a non-fiction dictator, the real thing?

One of the basic political qualifications, opportunism, was embedded in the upbringing. We were fed a historical tradition with Britain both as glorious victimiser – the global imperial pink – and plucky victimised isle, underdog victor of Agincourt and the Armada. World Empire or Little Britain, whichever fitted best with the fickle national mood. Our expedient relationship with history had been supplemented, since Orwell's day, with more recent but equally supple myths: the Blitz and Dunkirk and D-Day. *Keep Calm and Carry On.*

By the end of the seventies, these nationalist parables felt stretched, though the elastic attaching us to a triumphant past was yet to snap. The country was opening up to a more honest appreciation of Britain's status in the world (Correlli Barnett's *The Collapse of British Power*), which meant less deference paid to the injustice of traditional arrangements of privilege, including the private education system. At school from 1975, we grew up in the middle of this uncertainty, steeped in the old rules while the old regime was creaking. Describing his fictional school in *The Longest Journey*, E. M. Forster sees the 'short ladder between this education and the Anglo-Saxon hegemony of the globe'. The hegemony was over and the ladder flat on the ground, still there but with nothing to lean against, or to climb towards. What were we supposed to do with it? What were we actually for?

Despite provocations, our private comfort zone survived intact. We were curious, for example, about extra-curricular trends like punk rock, which happened during our school years. Safe behind our high walls it had to be worth a look, and Cameron became fond of The Jam. When The Jam found out (in 2008) Paul Weller was not impressed: 'I just think, "which bit didn't you get?".' None of it, really. We carried on as blithely as before. The only lasting legacy of punk on power was to accentuate hair as a medium of communication. We lived through the miners' strike, but that was in the North.

Our empire-tainted lust for glory glowed on, and safe Tory parliamentary seats lay waiting as they always had, to be occupied with minimal effort by people like us. In the past that had been enough, and we might have stayed relatively harmless if we hadn't gone looking for new ways to get our names in gold on the honours boards. Restless, out of time, insecure about our place in the world, glory-hunting was what we'd been educated to do, and by the new century tyro Conservatives had lost or never had the will to conserve, by essentially doing nothing. This was new.

Modern Tory governments always claim to believe in reform, and no one could say we were scared of disruption. For years we'd lived at school then home in a state of permanent instability, and our total institution schools were totalitarian in the spirit identified by Hannah Arendt, swearing as they did by 'the impudent, conceited idea that everything can be done and their contemptuous conviction that everything that exists is merely a temporary obstacle that superior organisation will certainly destroy'. Or as my school reports used to say: *With more application, nothing should stand in his way.*

According to Orwell in 1941, the English 'have never caught up with power politics'. 'The totalitarian idea that there is no such thing as law, there is only power, has never taken root.' Which was surprising, because that was how our childhood was shaped, as a series of lessons in the exercise of power. Yes sir, no sir, ✔ sir, ✘ sir. As for the law of the land – as it applied to thieving or underage drinking or actual bodily harm – we were exempt. In the words of the Warden to the parents, he preferred the in-house solution of an expulsion, which he called 'a purging if you like'. Strong individual leadership was the answer.

Boys privately educated in this period learned to accommodate the lunacy of total power. Any rights we had at home were dismissed at school, and we heard so often that fear and punishment were for our own good that we came to believe this was true. Rules were unquestionable – obedience was all that mattered, often to vague clauses that favoured the whims of authority.

A.　Boys are responsible for knowing the School Rules.

B.　Boys are subject to School Discipline wherever they are during term.

C.　A breach of courtesy or of common sense may be regarded as a breach of Discipline.

Compliance was more important than critical thinking – excellent training for backbench Members of Parliament – and no lie was untellable however hard to believe. *Dear Mummy and Daddy, I like it here.* In this darkness, submerged instincts and feelings could evolve over time into blind and redemptive ambitions for power. Like Phaeton, we lost any sense of our flaws: sun god, world king, Lord Protector of England. The conscience-less space left by a vacated self could be squatted by a dangerous idealism, or a dangerous nihilism. Or by both. Each temporary state of mind alternated to cover the other – we were bred in politics to the bone.

Only a boy educated at private school, separated from a wider sense of community as his training for prime minister, could be 'mad enough to discard all limited and local interests – economic, national, human, military – in favour of a purely fictitious reality in some indefinite distant future'. Hannah Arendt died forty-one years before Brexit. She wrote this sentence in the middle of a passage about the rise of the Nazi Party, as an example of a characteristic shared by totalitarian states of the twentieth century. On the surface their actions might seem like lunacy, but the general populace needed to be treated like children and told it was for the best, even as we had been told when refusing to let go of the car. However bad it feels, it's for our own good. Settle down and don't make a fuss and everything will turn out well.

Our denial of our own suffering meant that we were rarely deterred by the suffering of others. Emotional pain was a display of weakness to be overcome, and any upheavals we initiated hardly registered when compared to separating children from their parents. Separate the United Kingdom from a federation of independent states, or break up the Union itself; never did us any harm. In fact self-inflicted pain was the right thing to do, and had been for generations. We belonged to a caste who self-harmed by choice, in return for personal advancement.

These were the political influences of our formative years, and they made a dubious basis for running the country. Despite that, and the unmerited superiority of our attitudes, we ended up in charge. It was neither surprising nor fair, but whenever threatened we knew from England's red-white-and-blue history that 'patriotism is usually stronger than class hatred'. For Orwell this was already problematic, but the age of social media has spiced patriotism with xenophobia, and allowed racism to stage a comeback. By making feints in these other directions, class could be relegated to one of the lesser anxieties available for political manipulation.

But despotism couldn't happen here, not in Britain.

With my nose deep in *The Origins of Totalitarianism*, I see that in Brexit Britain some of Arendt's conditions for dictatorial rule look familiar. Lies and reality are confused; the stateless and refugees are treated with contempt; 'nothing perhaps illustrates the disintegration of political life better than this vague, pervasive hatred of everybody and everything'. But still. The Chief of Police is not among the most powerful public positions in the land, not in Great Britain, not yet.

In the meantime, to encourage the first growths of total power, it helps to have a collusive press who'll label critics and opponents as anti-British. This is a line of attack with which we feel intensely relaxed, because there's nothing more British than an unfair system of education. We can also find uses for privately educated historians who glorify the Empire and gaslight every other class: the historical greatness of Britain, by implication, depends on traditional social ascendancies.

Unfortunately, our schools left us ill-prepared for the Britain we felt entitled to lead. Hannah Arendt warns that 'a government will let evil spread if it knows the country is disintegrating in any case'. Released wide-eyed from our exclusive schools, we couldn't believe what Britain was like out there. Away from our mansions and chapels, the quads and the gang-mown playing fields, the rest of the country came as quite a shock. The kingdom was not united, and compared to the future-past we'd been promised, the alien in-between places of Britain were frankly appalling. Where was the spirit of Francis Drake? Where were the scones

235

and our holy past? We preferred our theme-park England of mortar boards and cricket flannels, and old Mr Chips ticking the dead off his register before supper in Hall. That was where we'd grown up, in our havens of fantasy Britain.

The criteria as itemised by Arendt threaten to come together. A selective historical memory allows a centralised state to connect with an atomised society. Set free from reality, an exceptionalist tribal nationalism unites a fractured country against a world of enemies, from European bureaucrats to a Chinese virus. The next step is to exploit crisis conditions, and in adversity the boarding school boys can be reliably and divertingly upbeat: we have extensive childhood experience at pretending, in any abnormal situation, that everything is perfectly fine. The hardship and emotional repression will finally pay off, because cometh the hour.

In such favourable circumstances, the right man from the right background might feel it his duty to offer the consolation of strong leadership, expecting opposition only from girly swots. During a crisis a supreme leader was what a country needed, to promise with abandon that Britain was on the verge of a bright new dawn. The glory that was, will be again, and we knew all about that: we'd gone to school in 1910, or thereabouts. As for the moral implications, in the right schools we'd always had a muddled set of standards, eroded from the moment adults called it 'right' to wave goodbye to your parents without showing emotion. Morality, in any case, was relative – we behaved one way at school and another at home. At school, like throughout the British Empire, truth and falsehood were contingent, or in Arendt's words, 'a matter of power and cleverness, of pressure and infinite repetition'.

If you didn't agree, then punishment was a fact of life – enforced silences, beatings, expulsions – the authoritarian monopoly of violence a form of power we recognised. It was in the air we used to breathe. Wayward individuals could be remodelled by absolute power, and bent to the will of the institution. Not us, not now, but we had our eye on anyone who embodied the vulnerability we refused to admit in ourselves. You wear the wrong clothes or shoes, or speak with an unacceptable accent. You look quizzically at the Union Jack, or fail to wear a poppy or you own a ukulele. Only we know the unspoken, internalised rules.

Compared to the childhood of Mussolini, however, or the childhood of Hitler, our schooldays would appear to leave villainous boxes unticked.

Up to a point. The German historian Volker Ullrich tries to understand Hitler's childhood in the context of the social forces that created him. Hitler's early life was 'a strange existence characterised by roles'. He had a 'bottomless mendacity' and 'wasn't even honest towards his most intimate confidants'. *'Are you crying?' 'No.'* Hitler lied to his friends and family, he lied to himself. *I love the house and the masters, the pupils and the Chapel. The Chapel especially.*

As a younger man Hitler was underestimated, and his career constantly threatened to come undone. He moved house frequently, and despite the hypothesis of dictator as frustrated artist, he was no better than average at painting. His canvases were the equivalent of an underachieved novel, a daub like *Seventy Two Virgins*. A stranger to self-doubt, Hitler dismissed his setbacks and continued to rise. He fancied himself an architect and envisioned a gigantic new bridge across the Danube. Fantasy bridges were psychologically important to these types of character, stranded as they were between divided selves. 'He cocooned himself in a bizarre, alternative world,' Ullrich writes, 'somewhere between dream and reality.'

Benito Mussolini's first English-language biographer was Christopher Hibbert, author of *No Ordinary Place: Radley College and the Public School System 1847–1947*. Write what you know, as they say in writing classes. It's from Hibbert I discover that in the counter-propaganda of the 1920s, Mussolini is always portrayed as 'a monstrous buffoon'. He is something like an eccentric teacher in an English public school, any time between then and the early 1980s. He postures, he speechifies. On the other hand, he was born the son of a blacksmith in the northern Italian village of Predappio, and even in prep school we ate better food than foraged radishes and chicory. Angry, experiencing privation, Mussolini as a child supposedly said: 'One day, I shall astonish the world.'

You too, Benito?

He wrote a novel, *The Cardinal's Mistress*, but alas 'not a very interesting book and certainly not a very lively one'. He became a journalist, and wasn't without talent – 'he is able to talk and write arrogantly about all the things that he knows nothing whatever about,' said Ignazio Silone in *The School for Dictators*. Whatever else Mussolini learned there, we were in that school too. Mussolini was famous

238

for being untidily dressed, and his personality cult was fuelled by boosterish optimism. He was resilient, despite multiple failures, and left rational observers baffled: 'his attacks were outlandish, his facts often wrong, his opinions usually contradictory, his attitudes theatrical'.

Mussolini the fascist in the making 'created an image, part fact and part fantasy, of a man of destiny natively cunning and widely learned'. All he need do was fool enough of the people enough of the time. 'If I were an Italian,' Churchill is reported to have said when visiting Rome in 1927, 'I would don the Fascist Black Shirt.' It therefore doesn't come as a surprise when a contemporary of Mussolini's, a sympathetic Italian journalist, looks at Il Duce and sees a classic public school boy: 'No one understands him. By turns shrewd and innocent, brutal and gentle, vindictive and forgiving, great and petty, he is the most complicated and contradictory man I have ever known. He cannot be explained.'

I think he can.

Stalin went to boarding school. In *Young Stalin*, the historian Simon Sebag Montefiore claims Stalin's early life 'equipped him (and damaged him) for the triumphs, tragedies and predations of supreme power'. Stalin's boarding school was the seminary in Tbilisi, the capital of Georgia, and given his own upbringing Sebag Montefiore (Ludgrove, Harrow) can't resist making the inevitable comparisons. Stalin was 'locked for virtually every hour of the day in an institution that more resembled the most repressive nineteenth century English public school than a religious academy'.

What Stalin certainly did learn at boarding school was the power of 'surveillance, spying, inversion of inner life, violation of feelings'. The brutal, insular plays for perks and preferment convinced him of the reductive notion that people were either for or against him, and by the end of his schooldays Stalin had adapted to hide his damaged self. His first step in adult life was familiar: he tried out an artistic career as a poet, but in his own words 'lost interest because it requires one's entire attention'. He became a journalist instead, of course he did, and seeded a personal mythology that invented, distorted and concealed the truth about who he really was.

In the 1930s, Stalin asked his mother why, as a child, he was beaten so frequently. She replied: 'It didn't do you any harm.'

What we know is that these mendacious, elliptical men were considered intelligent in their youth (Stalin, too, was a scholarship boy) and they all had a Christian education. In England we took these characteristics and added to them a sense of entitlement. We accepted we were educated to lead, one of Galsworthy's 'instincts of caste that forbid sympathy and understanding between the well-to-do and the poorer classes'. We were destined for power, nobody could deny it, and by virtue of that power we remained in power, where as latent dictators we had the edge in considering ourselves exceptional. Admittedly, it helped if the electorate wanted to believe in a great leader as unfailingly as we were confident we could provide one, to the point where a public school prime minister largely incoherent between his ums and errs could be hailed as a great communicator.

As was Hitler, as in his day was Mussolini.

These dictators were nothing special, not in the context of an English boys' boarding school. We were *all* going to be King of the World. How did I know? Because I was also exceptional in that way, and had the learned traits for tyranny. We were conditioned megalomaniacs, and in our fear of boy-on-boy hurt, physical and verbal, for years we inhaled the paranoia indispensable for success in this particular field. We were taught to think big, and to fake impregnable self-esteem, with the most susceptible among us mirroring the desire of Goebbels to have 'access to history, even at the price of destruction'.

In her biography Sonia Purnell calls Johnson 'an original – the opposite of a stereotype, the exception to the rule'. Not quite. He was any boy who started at boarding school in 1975, only more so because not growing up was openly a feature of his performance. He flaunted shamelessly what the rest of us tried to conceal: he was chaotic, unformed, cruel, slapdash, essentially frivolous. When he messed up he was just a boy, with his boyishly ruffled hair, and expected to be excused. An expert dissembler, he discovered the best place to hide was in plain sight.

Maybe I should have thought of that. Once, aged about fourteen or fifteen, with a dreary boarding school Sunday ahead of me, I walked out onto the empty expanse of the Radley College playing fields. There was the wooden hut about halfway out, and I intended to sit on the bench along the back wall, hands in my pockets and with a view of the school, staying there until I'd formulated, to my own satisfaction, a viable route from schooldays to British prime minister. Preferably by teatime. And maybe that's what I'd have done, if a boy called Pegg or Peck hadn't turned up with a rugby ball. We had a kickabout and I never nailed down the plan.

It therefore didn't surprise me when James Wood, the literary critic and another Eton contemporary of the two prime ministers, had this to say in the *London Review of Books*: 'None of us identified David Cameron as the boy marching inexorably towards Downing Street. When he became Tory leader in 2005, I had difficulty recalling him.' Even Cameron's Eton teachers, according to Sonia Purnell, claimed not to remember teaching him. The point is, any of us could have been prime minister. Anonymous Cameron, extrovert Johnson or thousands of us with our play-acted characters somewhere in between. Britain was organised to our advantage, but whatever individual pattern of camouflage we adopted we were concealing the same small boys, needy for love and approval.

We had boyish ambitions, like power without responsibility: we were failed men. The danger came when a failed man – his vanities, his insecurities – joined forces with a failed people. Our simplistic old school entitlement found a fit with a distracted, disillusioned populace: we had in common a patriotism that was more like homesickness, strongest in anyone who felt abandoned and unloved, without purpose in the wrong place at the wrong time. On these terms an alliance always threatened between the much too rich and the much too poor, with moderate stragglers left mystified in the shrinking middle ground.

14

Secrets and Lies

'I understood definitely that he [Cromwell] had blown up
all sorts of things and was therefore a very great man.'

Winston Churchill, *My Early Life*, 1930

Churchill is referring to the time in 1649 when Oliver
Cromwell used eleven pieces of heavy siege artillery
to pound the fortified Irish town of Drogheda. When
Cromwell's troops finally charged through the battered
walls they massacred an estimated two thousand people,
including some who'd surrendered and others who'd fled
for sanctuary into St Peter's Church, and were burnt alive
when English soldiers set the building alight.

The line is a joke, of course. Churchill adopts a vague,
amused distance from his observation, his irony imply-
ing he knows better without saying exactly how or why.

Laugh, move on. That's the way we do it. At the same time, Churchill's childish admiration (he writes this passage in *My Early Life* in the voice of the child he used to be) for the authoritarian Cromwell is allowed to remain intact. So much smoke, so many mirrors, all in a nod of acknowledgement from one all-powerful British commander-in-chief to another. This begs the question of what a modern supreme leader, if conditions aligned in his favour, would actually look like.

History has dispensed with Cameron now. He transmitted a dose of his public school damage to the body politic but he was weak, and in the end a bit of a weed. He didn't believe strongly enough in the land of hope and glory. We jeer and flick him with towels in the showers, and he whines *Don't you know who I am?* Not even his Eton teachers knew who he was. Which leaves Johnson, and whoever emerges next from the old school cloisters.

'A man ten times a failure, extremely lazy, incapable of steady work; a man who has spent long periods in institutions; a disappointed bohemian artist; a total good-for-nothing.' This is how Thomas Mann described Adolf Hitler in 1938, and the most unlikely looking candidates could rise to positions of prominence. All three of the twentieth century's pre-eminent dictators at first looked improbable. One too shrill, one too fat, one too Georgian, with the British consistently failing to spot the danger. The Etonian Foreign Secretary and former Viceroy of India, Lord Curzon, dismissed Mussolini with patrician scorn: 'He is really quite absurd!' We didn't then know the importance, as identified by Hannah

Arendt, of recognising when the ridiculous stops being ridiculous.

Luckily, Anglo-Saxons aren't Italians. We're certainly not Germans. We're special. We have our unique sense of humour, which allows for an overgrown boy – my age, my upbringing – with ill-fitting trousers and tousled hair to get as far as Downing Street with his own children barely in evidence and a dad shouting encouragement from the sidelines. Honestly, he would have us believe, none of this boyishness is relevant. He kept his thumbs up and his guard intact, always a sunny day on the platform at Canary Wharf, where stray colleagues could be nudged into agreeing that existence was ludicrously transient. The *Daily Telegraph* melted away – what a joke – and Canada Tower crumbled into its reflection in the Thames. If nothing was serious no one gets hurt, boarding school attitudes casually extended to London, the country, the world.

The register of Johnson's political bluster was close to mock-heroic, Molesworth as prime minister, with the added joke that some people didn't realise he was joking. Or was he? The candidate who Johnson beat to become Oxford Union president didn't think so, and warned others not to be deceived: 'This guy is an absolute fucking killer.' So Johnson had the advantage of surprise even though an ironic dictator, presumably, wouldn't be as dictatorial as a straight one. It was probably a mistake for both his friends and enemies to have accepted so early in his career that whatever he said, the opposite might be true.

His non-stop pantomime both exaggerated and obscured the class and the era that made him. When James Joyce identified Robinson Crusoe as an English archetype, he recognised an Empire schoolboy cut off from the known world, self-reliant but deprived of human connection. Crusoe subsisted alone on his island for years, but the writer Joseph Conrad, an immigrant who as a merchant seaman had first-hand experience of the British Empire, was less forgiving of our distinctive national traits. What happened to a lost and abandoned soul in contact with rival ideas of how to live? In *Heart of Darkness*, Crusoe's near namesake Kurtz is as emotionally isolated but also 'hollow to the core'. He is 'reckless without hardihood, greedy without audacity and cruel without courage'. Both these diagnostic novels were available in the school library and bookshop.

If Johnson missed out on the chance to read them, they add plausible later chapters to memories of his schooldays. In *Just Boris*, Sonia Purnell lifts a passage from Johnson's journalism, and given the man's education and reputation, his smoke and mirrors, she makes sure to state that on this occasion, unusually, she considers his reflections to be honest and believable:

'My memory of an otherwise idyllic 1970s English prep school is that masters used virtually any weapon of discipline they could lay their hands on.' He [Johnson] goes on to reveal an uncharacteristically heartfelt conviction: 'I remember being so enraged at being whacked for talking at the wrong moment that it has probably given me a lifelong distrust of authority.'

Note the casually ironic deflection of 'otherwise idyllic', meaning otherwise apart from the physical abuse of children. Many recollections of boarding school life follow this pattern: idyllic apart from the bedwetting and the emotional constipation and the phantom illnesses and the nightmares and the grief and homesickness on the first night back in uniform, on bare knees in a cold echoing chapel, surrounded by boys and alone. Apart from that, our schooldays were idyllic like Hogwarts, but instead of a background of magic we had sadism and sexual perversion and surveillance.

No wonder we have a distrust of authority. I have it myself. So what was likely to happen when we *were* authority? The nineteenth-century principles that informed our schools warped in contact with the late twentieth century, twisting into new psychological shapes: as an adult, Johnson stopped brushing his hair. He risked a gesture of rebellion left permanently on show, even when broadcasting on television from his own house, with hairbrushes presumably available, if required. In the spirit of his privilege Johnson was having his cake and eating it. He was prime minister, but on his own terms, which didn't necessarily include the maturity previously taken for granted.

From my inside knowledge of private schooling in the late seventies and early eighties, I'm fairly sure that building a thousand-year Reich wasn't what as schoolboys we had in mind. Nevertheless, these schools shouldn't be dismissed as minor sideshows in the nation's pageant of class.

In 1979, reality TV uncovered a more complicated reality at Radley College, and in true playground fashion Warden Silk attempted to deflect the blame for everything about *Public School* he disliked. We're not wrong, *you're* wrong. The BBC was an enemy, part of 'a world which has no love for the old establishment and its values', and the film's director had been placed under intolerable pressure. Silk invented a threatening, frightening BBC because threats and fear were what he knew: a closed world where few dared step out of line. This ruthlessness disguised by charm, the fist inside the palm, is a lesson in *How to be Topp*, the title of the second collection of Molesworth's fictional diaries. Never forget to disguise the ruthlessness. Self-deprecate. Waffle. Quote pointless Latin, whatever works.

But the combination of ruthlessness and dissembling isn't new, nor the dominance in British politics of boys from a rarefied background. In *Public School*, a late-night gathering of teachers sits gripped by the TV coverage of the 1979 general election: they want to know what will become of them. Eerily, the BBC commentary is voiced by David Dimbleby, in the same distinctive accent that announced the Cameron hung parliament in 2010 and the Brexit result in 2016. It's as if between these events nothing has changed, not even the identity of the BBC frontman, himself one of us as his father had been before him. And indeed his son after him, an Eton contemporary of Rees-Mogg who in 2018 as a non-political 'outsider' was appointed to the board of the Department for Environment, Food and Rural Affairs.

The game went on as it always had, and it was exactly *because* well-bred British leaders didn't take power too seriously that the nation was safe. Our essential dilettantism ensured British freedoms – we couldn't be bothered with absolute power because we didn't like to commit. Far too emotionally compromising. For a supreme leader to emerge, some other factor in Britain would have to change.

Not much obviously had, at least since Orwell's thoughts from the darkest days of the last century. We still elected our Parliament by an antiquated first-past-the-post ballot, and 'the English electoral system ... is an all but open fraud. In a dozen obvious ways it is gerrymandered in the interest of the moneyed class.' As for those in Parliament tasked with resisting the rise of over-strong leadership, 'one of the dominant facts in English life during the past three quarters of a century has been the decay of ability in the ruling class'. That was also us, business as usual with the same old boys haw-hawing on the plump green benches, quite capable of ignoring Orwell's rallying cry to 'fight against privilege, against the notion that a half-witted public schoolboy is better for command than an intelligent mechanic'.

In the twenty-first century, the half-witted schoolboys are as prominent as ever. Naturally they'd only allow a boy unmistakably from the caste – under-scrutinised, over-indulged – to endanger the structures and traditions that made us what we are. We could only be betrayed by one of our own, but what other kind of betrayal is there?

Modern Britain was not the place we'd been led to expect from our paid-for private distance in the 1970s.

Confronted by a confusing and threatening post-Empire reality, the lessons drummed into us as children could mutate into new and unnerving varieties of action. Like beta version supreme leaders, we contained most of the major features but weren't yet, subject to testing, ready for the full dictatorial rollout. Joy Schaverien identifies the basic unit of cruelty: 'They hide their feelings and, through projection, attack the child less able to hide theirs.' Along with a useful remoteness – our emotional dissociations, our social disdain – we might one day re-enact the political hustings of our youth by flirting with extreme solutions to a hostile and divided world where every difficult situation could be reduced to a simple binary choice. School or home, private or public, victimiser or victim, us or them. Give us the right emergency at the right time, and we'd know the right thing to do. We'd save the poor childish people of Britain from enemies they didn't know they had.

For this to work, a vocal minority of the public had to be persuaded along for the ride, which Umberto Eco includes among his preconditions for tyranny: 'the emotional response of a selected group of citizens can be presented and accepted as the Voice of the People'. The internet made this trick easier, but at first glance an unholy alliance remained implausible. Among other obstacles, like British common sense, there was the Latin. My 1980 diary is embarrassing with the boyish language of the times: *Aliquis latet error*, I write. Forty years later a prime ministerial candidate couldn't outgrow this childishness: *Salus populi suprema lex esto*, he said, in public. His Latin was a reminder of what kind of school he went to. It was a *canem sibilus*, a dog whistle summoning the old tribal allegiances, and, with any luck, the old ascendancies and habits of deference. Astonishingly, alarmingly, it worked.

Greatness was remembered and greatness was promised. It didn't have to be delivered, but this is what had changed. Orwell, finally, had fallen behind the times. In 1941, despite the falling bombs, he felt optimistic about the future because 'in England all the boasting and flag-waving, the "Rule Britannia" stuff, is done by small minorities. The patriotism of the common people is not vocal or even conscious.' He couldn't have known, in his blacked-out rooms, that the Second World War itself would change the nature of British patriotism. Since then we've had intravenous Spitfires and Union Jack branding on the tail lights of BMW-made Minis. A privately educated elite could invite a frustrated electorate to feel warm and welcome in a largely mythical past, just as we did, until it felt like sentimental nationalism was holding the country together. That was us, that was. Rah. England couldn't get enough of the boasting and the flag-waving, the stuff of Rule Britannia.

This was a start. The British public could be encouraged to share our delusions even when based on lies. From an early age, remember, we could deceive ourselves we weren't homesick, we were the next Winston Churchill, and as a designated great man Churchill could get away with anything. Near the beginning of *Young Winston* the actor Simon Ward intones a voiceover which has the cadences of a written Churchill passage, though I can't find the original source. Winston as a small boy is arriving at his prep school for the first time, and it helps to read these words in the fight-them-on-the-beaches voice:

> I paid for my sins, real or imaginary, in advance, because when I was but seven, I was cast out of my happy home and sent away to school.

This is a pithy explanation of our sense of entitlement. In our schooldays we suffered enough, suffered in advance, so that subsequently our moral debts were paid and we could do no wrong. Or if we did, we deserved to escape further punishment. Johnson remembers being 'whacked', but Sonia Purnell translates this bluster into language closer to the truth: 'he was confronted by the misery of beatings (and possibly worse)'. Thanks in part to the efforts of Alex Renton, one teacher from Ashdown House at that time has been jailed for sexual offences, and allegations of abuse have been made against six others. Even if it didn't visit us directly, paedophilia was in the air, both before and after evening chapel.

So all things considered, if repression failed, after a childhood like ours it would only be human to want to make a stand. As adults, every apparent misstep can be read as an act of resistance. I will not wait in line for lunch with my pumice-stoned hands outstretched. I will sing and whistle in the cloisters. I refuse to use my stipulated hairbrush and comb. Whoever we were when we arrived, boarding school remade us. That was the point, and a suppressed instinct for retaliation could later reappear with magnified consequences, especially when as adults we took back control. If I were the national headmaster, which I'm not, I'd want more from my power than conserving the country for the next crop of boys like me.

One day a petulant schoolboy with an upbringing similar to mine could wake up in Downing Street, his home from home, and feel empowered to do what he wanted. What he deserved. He was unlikely to stop at ruffling his hair before dominating his weaker classmates. If he considered himself special, if he believed he was exceptional, he might dare the outright tantrums of autocracy. And in England, if the country were ever to veer in that direction, look for the proximity of boys hurt and toughened by the hypocrisy of their schooling, with no outlet of escape to far-flung colonies, who were prepared to corrupt the traditions of public office with utter contempt for English respectability.

I could argue this position, if I chose to do so. English private schools could plausibly have bred a tyrant. I have the training to reason both for and against this argument, at the last minute opting for whichever conclusion might bring me the greater personal advantage.

And remember: being great doesn't mean being good. We had Carlyle's Great Man Theory of history in our bones, taught by parodic Great Man schoolmasters who agreed without hesitation that significant events – both inside the classroom and out – were inspired by exceptional and unique individuals. A boy educated in the classics could revere the Emperor Augustus for crushing democracy in favour of dictatorship, because a bookmarked place in history was his reward; it didn't matter what for. He was great *because* he was remembered, and our honed debating skills meant that no political figure was ever beyond redemption.

This house believes, contrary to the well-known poem, that King John was not not a good man. We could argue John's case, if it was a Wednesday, along with any other contrarian motion put before us. *This house believes that the British Empire should be a lasting source of national pride.* Down was up and wrong was right. For the exercise of tyranny, we were impeccably prepared. We'd grab the big cake and devour it to the last crumb.

Only I don't think this will happen. I don't honestly believe that small boys, some so young and helpless they can't brush their hair, can be expected to take on the full psychodrama of patricide. It isn't easy to kill a country, even one as old and frail as Britain, and whatever the after-effects of our education none among us had a youthful march on Rome or experience of trench warfare to sharpen our appetite for power. Stalin's school was not in fact much like an English public school – his headmaster was murdered and his drunken father, 'Crazy Beso', liked to hammer on the gates demanding money from his son.

Instead, now that we have power, the instinct at work is more secretive, less a direct assault and more like sabotage. To prolong our tribal dominance, we could choose to preserve the England that educated us and gifted us our posts and our prizes. Equally, as boys underprepared at the near-edge of an unbelievable past for a frankly baffling future, we might find more psychological satisfaction in letting the country slide.

All that privation had been for nothing. We were tough, sure, but in politics being amusing or cunning was just as relevant to survival. We felt cheated by the bleakness of the Lord is my Shepherd I Shall Not Want, lines we'd heard in short trousers in chapel without explanation, too young to understand. We did want. We wanted toys and pets and families and homes and love. Instead, we had years of total institutions whose theory of human nature had it that life was hard and only the toughened would flourish.

As one prescient TV critic wrote, reviewing *Public School* in 1980, 'What you do at a public school, it appears, is "to acquire the right habits for life", like Burgess and Maclean.' Guy Burgess and Donald Maclean were boarding school boys in positions of influence who passed British secrets to the Soviet Union between the 1930s and the 1950s, along with three fellow public school conspirators. One of these Cambridge spies, Anthony Blunt, worked for the Queen and had the code name 'Johnson'.

In *A Perfect Spy*, John le Carré's East German spymaster is surprised at how easy it is to run a conflicted English public school boy as a double agent against his own country:

All the junk that made you what you are; the privileges, the snobbery, the hypocrisy, the churches, the schools, the fathers, the class systems, the historical lies, the little lords of the countryside, the little lords of big business, and all the greedy wars that result from them, we are sweeping that away for ever. For your sake. Because we are making a society that will never produce such sad little fellows as Sir Magnus.

Such sad little fellows as me, and my short-trousered pals Cameron and Johnson, and 64 per cent of the Cabinet and over 50 per cent of the legal system, and the sad little fellows heading up the armed forces and the BBC and the established Church of England. We haven't been swept away, not yet, but we're not stupid. For us, it isn't enough to follow in the footsteps of the boys who've gone before. We were taught to look down on the grammar school prime ministers, the proles, the women, the blacks, the queers and the foreigners, so it can't be surprising if we hate what we've been taught to become. With power in our hands we could take revenge, little lords of the flies poking at fragile national structures, destabilising the stubborn traditions of England.

Set on making a difference, Orwell's simple remedy for the nation was the 'abolition of all hereditary privilege, especially in education'. We too wanted to make a difference, and if we still had the brains we were born with we'd refuse to settle for the status quo. The harder we wobbled the country the happier we were. If our education was worth anything at all, we somehow had to have learned that a society dependent for leadership on an educational system that favoured the wealthy was sick. We were sick with it ourselves. You'd have to be an idiot not to see the nonsense, the balderdash, the tommyrot, the piffle and waffle, the poppycock and whole caboodle. The absurd rules and uniforms, and the gross injustice of the old boy network, which was outrageously helpful and exactly as described: a social and professional safety net for boys who never grew up. Our England wasn't worth preserving, not the England that had made us what we were.

And however hard we shoved and rattled, everything would turn out well in the end. At least for us, because that was the life we knew and the outcome with which we were familiar. If in fact we succeeded in changing nothing, then the undisturbed rhythms of English privilege would continue to work in our favour, as they always had. On the other hand, if the poor old country started to fray and break, with former certainties swept away, then at last we'd have had our revenge. When we succeeded we failed, when we failed we succeeded. This is the people we are.

As for collateral damage, it was true that we could casually ruin everything, except our sheltered education had failed to teach us the full implications of 'ruin', or 'everything'. Whatever happened we as individuals would be fine, and not just because we had money. That was the extent of our experience, our psychological frontier. Apart from this significant limitation, and the manoeuvrings of our lost secret selves – *calculated and underhand* – we knew exactly what we were doing. Trust us.

15

Home

'Intellectual, spiritual, and artistic initiative is as dangerous
to totalitarianism as the gangster initiative of the mob, and
both are more dangerous than mere political opposition.'
Hannah Arendt, *The Origins of Totalitarianism*, 1951

After 1933, Hitler arranged for the confiscation of all
private documents that revealed information about
his childhood and youth. Stalin was so protective of the
facts of his early life that even his birthday was a mystery.
In the worst-case scenario for understanding this phase of
English history, the reality of private schools in the period
that bred our leaders will be lost. Heatherdown closed in
1982. On 1 June 2020, Ashdown House announced its clo-
sure with a statement on the school website. In a gesture
of unassailable snobbery, or for some other reason, there

was never any mention on the site that the current prime minister was once a boy at the school.

'We take some solace from the fact that, while the school is unable to continue, Ashdown's impact will be felt for generations to come.'

It certainly will.

At best, our boy-men leaders will be too ironic for demagoguery. Our facetiousness – our self-conscious smarts, our superior disdain – will deter us from taking the deep English darkness too seriously. That's a position our education allows us to take, and any sustained crisis will find us out. In our mock-heroic posturing, the heroic is the least reliable component. Molesworth the Great Leader. Chiz. The durable British spirit will absorb the folly of this generation of public school twits as it has so many others before them.

Don't worry about us. We left a door open, so we could slip out the side. Cameron retreated from his days at Number Ten personally unscathed. He turned his back on the mess he'd made with the serenity of a public school boy whose ancestors had been public school boys too. Between the lectern and the door of his temporary grace-and-favour home Cameron hummed a happy tune. Thank you and goodnight. He'd been a bit naughty but no harm done, because the arrangements to protect his interests were securely in place. Or as my dad said in the Jag, driving his cast-out son away from the school and back to Swindon: *We'll say no more about it.*

I'm saying something now.

In the poems we memorised at school we made allowances for public school leaders whose careers peaked at shameful, ridiculous disaster. At the avoidable Charge of the Light Brigade *Someone had blundered / Theirs not to make reply, / Theirs not to reason why*. In modern politics, moments of blundering seem less likely to pass with insufficient reasoning why, but in Britain private education should be high on the list of reasons. If our studied flippancy saves us from ourselves, and we baulk at outright tyranny, then that's mainly through fear of looking ridiculous. In the end we can't take anything seriously, not even 'world king', our earliest stated ambition. On the other hand, gifted an opportune crisis, a spot of despotism might keep us entertained while winding up the socialists.

Nobody can say they weren't warned. By 1947 George Orwell was telling anyone who'd listen that 'the characteristic faults of the English upper and middle classes may be partly due to the practice, general until recently, of sending children away from home as young as nine, eight or even seven'. The practice was still going strong in the 1970s, and forty years later the result is a wasted decade and a half of defective leadership, as if the emotional injury of a boarding school education was still a national mystery. Churchill himself saw this dispossession for what it was, nearly a century ago in *My Early Life*. Instead of being sent away to school, he'd have preferred to stay at home with his family. 'It would have been real; it would have been natural, it would have taught me more; and I should have done it much better. Also I should have got to know my father, which would have been a joy to me.'

Aged thirteen, in my 1980 diary, I identified the basic problem: *In some ways I am a sort of scitzophrenic. With two sides to my character*. We weren't even a mystery to ourselves. Even at the time we appreciated that the flaw in English private schooling was its production of English private schoolchildren. It couldn't yield anything else, creating for the future a tribal loyalty that superseded empathy across barriers of gender and class and race. In the context of our seventies and eighties education we were not dysfunctional: we were the intended premium product.

In Thomas Mann's words, those of us who failed to escape our education were ideally placed to learn 'the fundamental arrogance which thinks itself too good for any sensible and honourable activity'. *Fuck business*, as if Britain's economy was like 'trade' in the nineteenth century, to be despised from up above. But lurking beneath that arrogance, 'the bad conscience, the sense of guilt, the anger at everything, the revolutionary instinct, the unconscious storing-up of mines of compensatory wishes'. We too had that spaghetti of mixed emotions, like the worst of the twentieth-century bad guys.

All we ever wanted, however high a position we achieved, was to be allowed back home. When this simple, primitive, powerful urge was disregarded we found ourselves stranded neither here nor there, and Britain was condemned by tradition to be run by men of arrested development. Unless we could contrive an escape, the newspaper editors and judges and ministers and generals, among so many others in positions of power, would continue to act like boys at boarding school. We lived for exeats and brexits, for getting out and getting away, scared little children for life.

Time to go home now.

The thread that unites the Britain of the 2020s with 1920 and 1820 is Orwell's famous definition of the country as 'a family with the wrong members in control'. If none of the wrong honourable members have so far acted on that warning, it's because happy families aren't our area of expertise. Being in control was always more important to us. Orwell hoped that war would be the great disruptor, now that 'the whole English-speaking world is haunted by the idea of human equality'. Post-war, with boarding schools as boot camps in social and emotional pragmatism, some of us stopped being haunted. The shameless inequality championed by the private schools proved amazingly resilient, and by celebrating this injustice as a jewel of British national life we signalled that other injustices too would always have their chance.

The schools themselves were seasoned at absorbing criticism. They could belittle it – *calm down, dear* – or simply ignore it. The documentary *Public School*, which in the opinion of Christopher Hibbert made the headmaster look 'unctuous' and the star teacher a 'buffoon' and the chaplain 'condescending', was shown for many years on a loop at the school's annual Open Day. For a laugh, presumably, and a shrug of indifference: time had moved on and everything was different now.

Skools are not what they were in my day, boys are no longer cruel to each other and the masters are friends.

From dads to sons, from teachers to boys, boarding school men handed on their arsenal of weapons for use in emotional self-defence. *My dear boy.* From the start of our schooldays, if we had any complaints, we were trained to *get over it*. The same was true at the end, after we left. *Moving on* was our way of saying we couldn't stand to talk about it. *Get a grip*. No one likes a moaner. Roald Dahl once watched his friend in the sickbay having a boil cut out with a scalpel, no anaesthetic, while Matron reminded both of them of their obligations: *Don't make such a fuss about nothing*. Don't cry out. Don't say anything. Schooldays were to be endured, and with luck had no lasting influence. But that couldn't be right, because we were supposed to turn to our advantage the best education money could buy (as if we had the first clue about education money *couldn't* buy).

In the past, if anyone complained, no one listened. Orwell's biographer Bernard Crick is dismissive: 'no terrible harm seems to have been done, as he himself claimed; or if some harm there was, it was not as black as he painted it'. Nor, presumably, as black as the pictures Orwell paints in the novels *Animal Farm* and *1984*. Orwell had no shortage of early-life lessons in blackness, but Churchill's hedged criticism was about as far as we were supposed to go: 'I am all for the Public Schools but I do not want to go there again.' This fate was reserved for our children, because unsurprisingly our lack of empathy also applied to the young, including our own.

If asked, say that everything was fine. *Dear Mummy and Daddy*. Or admit it wasn't perfect, but that you recognise your parents wanted what at the time they thought was best for you, the best education available. Make yourself sound as grown up as possible. *I know all the vowels and*

I am Quite interested in deer. Do not sneak. Do not write two hundred pages of *sneak*.

In other circumstances, say in a normally function-ing community, sneaking on other boys would alert the grown-ups that something was wrong and required atten-tion. But the grown-ups of my age in positions of authority – judges, lawyers, senior police officers, politicians – don't need to be told because they already know. They were at these schools like I was. Defended by their habits for life and protected by ambition they move on, and they move on, desperately keeping ahead of the shame and sadness and fear and anger. No wonder they don't look back.

I'm sneaking because I'm ashamed, sad, afraid and angry. I looked back, which just goes to show: not really prefect material.

We said: *I didn't choose to be sent to this kind of school.* Of course we didn't – what child can sensibly make a decision to leave home at the age of eight? But our lack of choice didn't cancel out the consequences, either the advantages or the injuries. With the benefit of hindsight, in our gener-ation the damage done disqualified us from leadership: our early life equipped us not for the responsibilities but only the predations of power.

'School,' says Mr Pembroke in E. M. Forster's *The Longest Journey* (and Mr Pembroke is a career schoolmas-ter, a gowned buffoon), 'school is the world in miniature.' Not in the 1970s it wasn't, not at a boarding school iso-lated from 95.5 per cent of the population, where boys untouched by the influence of parents or women lived out the last days of Empire shrunk into a scatter of country houses. With an upbringing like that, if we ever had the opportunity – and frankly the opportunity was always going to come our way – we couldn't be expected to make the best decisions for the greater good.

Hannah Arendt, an adult in the room, identified the problem a long time before we saw it for ourselves. Well into the twentieth century, Britain could console itself that whatever their faults, for many of these schoolboys 'their madness had remained a matter of individual experience and without consequences'. She means that from the eighteenth century onwards large numbers of us were out of sight out of mind, adventuring in India or Africa, not that our adventures were without consequences for the Indians and Africans.

Back in England at the heart of government, embedded in this and other vital organs of state, we risked spreading the virus far and wide. We were faking it, so we assumed everyone else must be faking it too. We judged that every person we met was frightened and self-protecting and had a guard to drop, as if everyone alive was a private school boy from the late 1970s. What you saw was never what you got. We projected defences onto others that in our experience were often necessary and routinely deployed, and always we needed a victim for our bullying and scapegoating to make sure it wasn't us. However brutal our attitudes, however loveless or ignorant or spiteful, we captioned our errors as the 'right thing to do'.

The right thing to do, it seemed, was never to stop and consider the vast unacknowledged silt of grief deposited forty years ago in the hearts of small children allocated an iron-framed bed in a dormitory. I've spent half a life-time enacting the fantasy escapes we dreamed of as boys: run for the hills, marry a foreign princess, if all else fails keep scraping out those tunnels. I've played a lot of organised sport. I've lived outside England, hoping the English past wouldn't follow. At various times I've retreated into a fortified position as an authority on holy relics or the iconography of Lazarus. With more patience I could have hidden for a lifetime behind forbidding expertise in the Roman Republic or eighteenth-century Dutch ceramics. And I'd have said: praise be, look what my education has allowed me to achieve.

As a small consolation, wherever I am and whatever troubles I'm acting out, at least I'm not prime minister. I didn't make that basic mistake. Nor did I kill myself. I can come out now, to escape from the 'we'. Treatment and recovery is possible, and it's all right to get help for this – for everyone's sake it's time that boys like me accepted we're not as tough as we thought. And we're not always right, and don't always know the right thing to do, simply because we went to the right schools. Instead, we hold the country back in a half-remembered era of Empire and the horse and cart, our leadership in its wisdom often pushing the cart out first.

We could do worse than to feel a little sorry for our-selves, as a first step towards learning to feel sorry for others. Let's break our habits for life, and as a default response to strangers reach not for ridicule but for kind-ness and understanding. George Orwell, and others like him, were exposed by the wars of the twentieth century to a seriousness that grew their stunted selves and tempered the isolated and ironic cult of an English private education. His generation were goaded by events into compassion, so that sooner or later, Orwell believed, even in 'a land of snobbery and privilege, ruled largely by the old and silly', England would brush aside the obvious injustice of the public schools.

Later, as it happened, so much later that the wait goes on. In 1979, I wasn't wrong that private school Conservatives looked unqualified for power; I hope I was just early. And forty years on, assuming the country survives Brexit and Covid, a more enlightened nation might look back on Cameron and Johnson as the Topp toff supernova, a final bright flare and a burning out, the dying of the public school light in a burst of corruption and incompetence so spectacular the glimmer will be visible from space.

Anyone betting on that outcome, at any point in the last six hundred years, would have lost. Up at Radley College, the tennis courts are open to resident staff and middle-aged men can again play golf. In sunshine the bicycle boy rides loops round Clock Tower and Shop. He sings his songs. He rings his bell. He isn't as old as I thought, and not very much is wrong with him. He's taking advantage of the empty school, and feeling joyful and free in the summertime.

My adult theory of human nature is not the version I was taught in my schooldays, with toughness as both a reward and a preparation for hardship. I now think that everything is in the past, even what hasn't happened yet. I'm still here at this school. We all are, although the others not as literally.

267

To replicate an incident from forty years ago, I wait for a Sunday to consider stepping away from the authorised footpath to cross the cricket outfields in the direction of the wooden hut. I'd hoped that at the weekend the groundsmen wouldn't be working, but it seems they are. At the far edge of the playing fields a tractor and trailer goes to and fro, but for nearly five years I've been living in Radley village without permission; presumably that's also against the rules.

GENERAL RULES
13. Boys, other than school prefects, may not walk across the mown lawns.

I step onto the grass and the bell in the clock tower chimes behind me – half past the hour. My heart beats faster with the buzz of transgression. I can't help it: my education is inside my body. A woman with a dog is crossing the grass towards me – a teacher, a teacher's wife – but she keeps herself socially distanced. I'm one of us, and I know what to do. Front up with confidence. I raise my hand to acknowledge her, and conspicuously avoid walking on the cricket squares. No one shouts, no one stops me.

The wooden hut is open on the side facing the school. Inside are two black wheelie bins, and along the back and side wall are wooden benches beneath a row of pegs. The building has a corrugated-metal roof, a concrete slab floor and on the back wall a simple wooden plaque: *In Memoriam, R. L. C. Southam, Radley, 1931–1950.* My beating heart spins a tragic tale of a nineteen-year-old life prematurely lost, but when I check later these are the years that Robin Southam, 'an extremely large and exuberant man', known to cry at showings of the film *Little Lord Fauntleroy*, was a teacher and housemaster at the school. He died suddenly, and the plaque remembers not a complete life, but his life in the time he was here.

I sit on the bench against the far wall, and stretch out my legs in front of me as I scan at a distance the red-brick buildings of the school. I'm further away than I remembered, further than the hut and copse look from the other direction. The school buildings appear to me ineradicable, a solid feature in the skyline of the future, just as they are of the past. The traffic noise from the A34 is up again in volume, I notice, and although I can hear chirruping in the trees round the hut, birdsong is once more background to the background noise. Up in the blue summer sky, a single contrail from a jet plane. Time moves on; life resumes. From my pocket I take out a pad and pen, in case anyone comes by and asks. This is why I'm here. This is what I'm for.

One Sunday afternoon, during my early teenage years, my prime ministerial career started and ended in this pavilion. It is amazingly peaceful in here, with the wind in the leaves of the beech trees. I think of that boy and his inflated expectations, believing it was high time he set in place his plans. Except he didn't come here to plot a route – the journey from here to Westminster was a path well travelled – but to decide whether that was the road he wanted to take. I find I'm glad that on that specific Sunday I was distracted by a boy with a rugby ball. I was the distractible type, and they hadn't educated that out of me.

I walk back the long way, over to the golf course and round the far edges of the pitches, none of it public-footpathed. If these schools are here in another forty years' time, fulfilling the same function, training segregated prime ministers, what a desperately sad outcome that would be – for the leaders and the led, for the enduringly disunited kingdom. Orwell had much the same fear:

> We cannot be certain that school, at any rate boarding school is not still for many children as dreadful an experience as it used to be. Take away God, Latin, the cane, class distinctions and the sexual taboos, and the fear, the hatred, the snobbery and the misunderstanding might still all be there.

Hand over the colours, give up the flag. The war is over. Let the British square break, and hope that at night in fevered dreams our demons – the Great Qing and the sepoys, Boers and the Mau Mau and so many others – take mercy on our reformed modern souls. I do not believe in England, not as led by boys like me.

Go home. Love, and allow yourself to be loved in return.

I can say with precision what I took away from this school when I left at the age of seventeen. The 1960 Bodley Head edition of *Ulysses*, which I stole from the Wilson Library. Wilson was a Warden from the late nineteenth century known as 'Zulu', a dark-complexioned teetotaller who was publicly hissed by the boys for placing bars across the windows to enforce a night-time curfew. James Joyce, author of *Ulysses*, aided and abetted my escape – I have the novel here on my desk. It is my favourite hardback book, with Joyce's approved cover design, deep blue with the letters of the title in white, like adjacent islands in the Aegean.

Back at the public footpath, I complete the final stage of my rescue. I join hands with my younger self and together we walk away, through the memorial arches and down the drive, past the lodge and the gates, out of the school. We'll read books, move house, grow vegetables, fall in love, see a therapist, spend that inheritance wisely, or not. It is possible, I believe, to break the chain of infection. We're going home.

Bibliography

Arendt, Hannah, *The Origins of Totalitarianism* (1951)
Beard, Alan, *Beard: 125 Years of Construction 1892–2017* (2019)
Beard, Richard, *Muddied Oafs* (2003)
    – *The Day That Went Missing* (2017)
Brendon, Vyvyen, *Prep School Children: A Class Apart Over Two Centuries* (2009)
Cameron, David, *For the Record* (2019)
Churchill, Winston S., *My Early Life: A Roving Commission* (1930)
    – *A History of the English-Speaking Peoples* (1956)
Crick, Bernard, *George Orwell: A Life* (1980)
Dahl, Roald, *Boy: Tales of Childhood* (1984)
Dudding, Richard, with Joyce Huddleston, Clare Sargent and Christine Wootton, *Radley Manor and Village, A Thousand Year Story* (2019)
Duffell, Nick, *The Making of Them: The British Attitude to Children and the Boarding School System* (2000)
    – *Wounded Leaders: British Elitism and the Entitlement Illusion* (2014)
    – and Thurstine Basset, *Trauma, Abandonment and Privilege: A Guide to Therapeutic Work with Boarding School Survivors* (2016)
Eco, Umberto, 'Ur-Fascism', *New York Review of Books*, 22/06/1995
Forster, E. M., *The Longest Journey* (1907)
    – *Maurice* (1971)

Fraser, George MacDonald, *Flashman: From the Flashman Papers 1839–42* (1969)

Goffman, Erving, *Asylums: Essays on the Social Situation of Mental Patients and Other Inmates* (1961)

Graves, Robert, *Goodbye to All That* (1929)

Greene, Graham, *England Made Me* (1935)

– (ed.), *The Old School: Essays by Divers Hands* (1934)

Hensher, Philip (ed.), *Molesworth* (1999)

Hibbert, Christopher, *Benito Mussolini: The Rise and Fall of Il Duce* (1962)

– *No Ordinary Place: Radley College and the Public School System 1847–1997* (1997)

Hickson, Alisdare, *The Poisoned Bowl: Sex, Repression and the Public School System* (1995)

Hilton, James, *Goodbye Mr Chips* (1934)

Hyam, Ronald, *Empire and Sexuality: The British Experience* (1990)

le Carré, John, *A Perfect Spy* (1986)

Low, George (ed.), *The Dirty Dozen: The Best 12 Commando Comic Books Ever!* (2005)

– *True Brit: The Toughest 12 Commando Comic Books Ever!* (2006)

Mann, Thomas, 'That Man is my Brother', *Esquire*, 01/01/1939

McTague, Tom, 'Boris Johnson Meets His Destiny', *The Atlantic*, 22/07/2019

Motion, Andrew, *In the Blood* (2006)

Orwell, George, *The Road to Wigan Pier* (1937)

– *1984* (1949)

– 'The Lion and the Unicorn: Socialism and the English Genius' (1941)

– 'Why I Write' (1946)

– 'Such, Such Were the Joys' (1952)

Purnell, Sonia, *Just Boris: A Tale of Blond Ambition* (2011)

Renton, Alex, *Stiff Upper Lip: Secrets, Crimes and the Schooling of a Ruling Class* (2017)

Schaverien, Joy, *Boarding School Syndrome: The Psychological Trauma of the 'Privileged Child'* (2015)

Sebag Montefiore, Simon, *Young Stalin* (2007)

Sutton Trust and Social Mobility Commission, *Elite Britain 2019* (2019)

Turner, David, *The Old Boys: The Decline and Rise of the Public School* (2015)

Ullrich, Volker, *Hitler: Volume 1: Ascent* (2013)

Verkaik, Robert, *Posh Boys: How the English Public Schools Run Britain* (2018)

Wakeford, John, *The Cloistered Elite: A Sociological Analysis of the English Public Boarding School* (1969)

Warner, Rex, *English Public Schools* (1945)

Watkins, Paul, *Stand Before Your God* (1993)

Waugh, Evelyn, *Decline and Fall* (1928)
   - *A Little Learning* (1964)

Willans, Geoffrey, and Ronald Searle, *Down with Skool!* (1953)
   - *How to be Topp* (1954)
   - *Whizz for Atomms* (1956)
   - *Back in the Jug Agane* (1959)

Wood, James, 'These Etonians', *London Review of Books*, 04/07/2019

Worsley, T. C., *Flannelled Fool: A Slice of a Life in the Thirties* (1967)

Acknowledgements

I'm indebted to Tim Beard and Sophie Walker, who responded with enthusiasm and tact to an early draft of this book, and to Peter Rich, Edward Rich and Lucy Blinko for sending on their recollections to jog my memory about Pinewood. For helping to navigate the more hidden regions of the past I'm grateful to Julian Masters. I'd also like to thank Sally Lines, 'Ravi' and my mum for their openness and generosity in response to my unsolicited questions.

In the ongoing present, I love Arthur, Maud and Eugene Beard none the less for their reliable feedback on my behaviour, and increasingly on my writing. I'm also lucky to have friends with expertise in specialist areas. Many thanks to James Holland for Hitler, Tom Holland for Latin, Barbara Kavanagh for Ireland, Dru Marland for birds and trees, Jonathan Wilson for football and Jon Hotten for his unattributed joke at the cricket. Still makes me laugh.

Lucy Luck continues to be the finest of agents, an unwavering source of confidence and support, while these pages were immeasurably improved by the unrivalled editing skills of Stuart Williams. I'd like to thank Stuart and everyone at Harvill Secker, in particular Mikaela Pedlow, for continuing to work to such high standards despite the challenging circumstances of the various lockdowns.

Any errors of judgement that remain are mine.